Collins

ROCKS AND MINERALS

ADRIAN JONES

Collins

Reprinted in 2012 for
Independent Book Sales

HarperCollins Publishers Ltd.
77-85 Fulham Palace Road
London W6 8JB

Collins is a registered trademark of
HarperCollins Publishers Ltd.

13 12
11 10 9 8 7

ISBN-13: 978 0 00 778538 4

Typeset and designed by D & N Publishing
Colour reproduction by Colourscan, Singapore
Printed and bound in China by South China printing company

HOW TO USE THIS BOOK

This book describes and illustrates 220 of the commoner minerals and rocks in Europe. Each specimen has a separate page carrying a clear colour photograph of its ideal form, as found in a professional collection, such as in a museum or university. For each specimen there is an ID Fact File listing its key features, which will help you to make an accurate identification. The accompanying text provides a brief description of the specimen, with points of interest, additional aids in identification and some basic indication of how the mineral or rock is formed or where in Europe and throughout the world it is known to occur.

The different mineral and rock groups are dealt with in the following order. Individual specimens within each group appear alphabetically.

Minerals

Rocks

Rocks will normally bear a close resemblance to the photographs. Owing to their natural variability in size and form, many minerals may differ considerably from their photographs. However, all is not lost, because minerals have distinctive crystal shapes, colours and nearly constant physical properties which can be tested. When all of their features are considered together, it is usually possible to identify most minerals when they are presented as a hand specimen. Some minerals are just very difficult to identify or to distinguish one from another, even for the experts, and definitive tests usually require laboratory chemical analysis. There are some suggestions on pp.11–12 for further resources and contacts.

Minerals represent specific concentrations of chemical elements, and many are used as the primary source of chemicals. The vast majority of minerals are harmless, and very few have sufficient concentrations of toxic elements, or some other unique hazard, to warrant caution when handling them repeatedly; avoid inhaling or tasting minerals with your tongue!

MINERALS

Minerals are naturally occurring chemical elements or compounds with a specific composition enabling them to be classified according to their chemical group (eg hydrous silicate) or family name (eg mica). For each mineral, information about the family name, chemical group and composition is given at the top of the page. In addition, all minerals possess a set of distinctive characteristics or properties that can aid identification. The following pages describe the most important identifying features for minerals and the terms that are commonly used in the Fact File.

Nearly all minerals have unique crystalline structures and they often occur with characteristic shapes or forms. All minerals belong to one of seven **crystal systems**, which describe the internal symmetry in the arrangement of their component atoms or molecules as mirrored frequently in their external development of crystal faces. The crystal system to which each mineral belongs is indicated by a symbol in the top left-hand corner of the page, as well as named in the Fact File. Additional artwork shows for each mineral the crystal shape for ideal crystals. The illustrations shown below represent the seven principal crystal systems.

The **colour** of many minerals is distinctive, whereas many may also show a wide variety of colours. Use only the colour

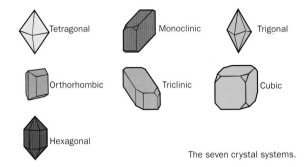

The seven crystal systems.

of a freshly broken surface. Many sulphide and other metallic minerals often develop a surface tarnish, which differs from the true colour but may also be useful for identification purposes.

The **form** in which a mineral occurs is an attempt to describe in an intuitive way its most obvious physical appearance. The main categories include whether or not individual crystal shapes are likely to be observed (crystalline), as solitary crystals or in groups (aggregates), the shapes of the crystals (equant, fibrous, radiating, etc). Commonly, large masses may occur with no individual crystal definition (massive) or with many small crystals (granular).

Cleavage is the way some minerals split along planes of weakness related to the molecular structure and parallel to possible crystal faces. The perfection of the cleavage describes in a qualitative way how well developed it is, from imperfect (as in apatite) through good to perfect (as in mica).

Hardness is used in an approximate way to identify minerals according to Moh's scale of hardness (*see* overleaf). For example, flourite is harder than calcite and less hard than apatite. If an unknown mineral will scratch all the minerals in the scale up to 4 and is scratched by 5 its hardness is somewhere between 4 and 5. Check carefully that there is really a scratch and avoid testing on valuable crystals! Some convenient standards to use in the field include fingernail (2.5), penny coin (3), steel penknife (5.5), window glass (5.5) and hardened steel file (6.5).

Relative and absolute hardness scale

Moh's hardness	Comparison mineral	Simple means of testing hardness	Absolute hardness
1	Talc	Easily scratched with fingernail	0.03
2	Gypsum	Can be scratched with fingernail	1.25
3	Calcite	Can be scratched with copper coin	4.5
4	Fluorite	Easily scratched with knife	5.0
5	Apatite	Can be scratched with knife	6.5
6	Orthoclase	Can be scratched with steel file	37
7	Quartz	Scratches window glass	120
8	Topaz		175
9	Corundum		1,000
10	Diamond		140,000

Specific gravity (SG) is the relative weight of a mineral compared to the weight of an equal volume of water (and is a dimensionless equivalent to density). SG can be estimated with practice and varies significantly. For example, sulphur and halite are low (2–2.1), compared with common calcite and quartz (~2.7), while sulphides like pyrite (~5) and native metallic elements like copper (~9) and gold (~19) can be very high.

Lustre depends on the resorption, reflection or refraction of light by a fresh surface of the mineral. Several mostly self-explanatory terms are used: adamantine (brilliant) like diamond; metallic (like metal) like galena; vitreous (glassy) like quartz; also, greasy, pearly, silky, earthy or dull. More than one lustre term indicates the range shown by different forms of that mineral.

Transparency is the degree to which light passes through a mineral, and ranges from transparent like quartz, through translucent like apatite to opaque (no light passes through) like pyrite.

Other simple physical tests listed vary from mineral to mineral, but often include **fracture**, a description of the surfaces when the mineral is broken, for instance when hit with a hammer; it may be conchoidal (shell-like) like quartz, hackly, uneven or brittle. The **streak** describes the colour of the powdered mineral when rubbed against a piece of unglazed white porcelain. Many carbonates react with dilute hydrochloric acid by fizzing and releasing bubbles of gas (carbon dioxide).

Additionally very few minerals are magnetic, like magnetite (which is very common), or strongly radioactive like uraninite (which is uncommon or rare). Finally for many minerals, lookalikes give a suggestion of which minerals may share similar properties or appearance to the one listed.

Where indicates within which broad classification of rocks (*see* next section) the mineral is likely to be found, and could be used in conjunction with a geological map. **Abundance** gives a rough idea of how common the mineral is in general, though of course at specific locations, like mines or quarries, this has reduced meaning; rock-forming is the most abundant where the mineral occurs in major, bulk quantities. Other terms are self-explanatory; abundant, common, uncommon, restricted, rare.

ROCKS

Rocks are large masses of material making up the Earth's crust; many are not solid, like soil and gravel. A rock may consist of just one mineral, like quartz, dolomite or calcite. Some rocks do not have discrete minerals but are made of glasses. However, most rocks contain several minerals, or were formed from older rocks where these minerals were present. The scientific study of rocks is called petrology. The main classification of rocks is based on their fundamental origin. **Igneous** rocks solidify from molten rock, called magma, which is emplaced into and onto the crust during volcanic activity. **Sedimentary** rocks are formed at the Earth's surface by weathering of older rocks or by chemical accumulations, some of which are associated with prolific biological activity. **Metamorphic** rocks are formed by the transformation of older rocks in response to high pressures and high temperatures either during crustal mountain building or adjacent to massive cooling bodies of igneous magma. The approximate volume proportions of these three rock types throughout the Earth's crust are: igneous rocks 65%; metamorphic rocks 27%; sedimentary rocks 8%. A fourth rock category is **meteoritic** rocks, which are rare extraterrestrial rocks including very rare fragments derived from the Moon and from Mars; they share some features of all three terrestrial rock types.

Igneous Rocks

All igneous rocks are derived from magma which forms by melting of the Earth's interior (the upper mantle); they are by far the commonest type of rocks in the Earth's crust. When this fluid magma intrudes the crust and cools very slowly, coarse crystal textures develop in coarse-grained plutonic rocks. If the magma is erupted through volcanoes onto the Earth's surface the same material is called lava; lava often cools down very quickly to form rocks with very small crystals, or fine-grained igneous rocks often containing glass. With few exceptions, igneous or magmatic rocks have compositions based on silica (SiO_2). The total silica content of an igneous rock expressed as a percentage of silica, gives one of four possible categories of chemical group for igneous rocks; acid (>66%), intermediate (52–66%), basic (44–52%) and ultrabasic (<44%). Classifications for igneous rocks rely primarily on the nature and proportions of their constituent minerals (or glass), and additionally on the relationship between their minerals, or their texture.

The igneous rocks are arranged into groups of coarse-grained, fine-grained and volcanic rocks. The key features are listed for each igneous rock under the ID Fact File, starting with a list of **essential minerals** that should be present, and a variety of other minerals which may also be present. The **mineral proportions** are listed in terms of priority; this is considered sufficient for identifications in this book, since more scientific classifications are highly quantitative and usually require additional examination of a specially prepared thin rock slice, under a polarised-light geological microscope.

Textural features can often be very helpful in identifying a rock; the textures are described avoiding technical terms wherever possible, and can usually be discerned using a hand lens.

The **distribution** of the rock indicates the style or form of the igneous rock; coarse-grained varieties, like gabbro, form large intrusions or plutons which can extend for kilometres, medium-grained igneous rocks like dolerite, form in relatively shallow sheet-like minor intrusions called sills (nearly horizontal) or dykes (nearly vertical), usually metre-scale widths. Volcanic rocks frequently contain glass and may record shattered crystals and other evidence of violent eruptions; remember steep sided volcanoes are much more dangerous than low shield volcanoes.

The **abundance** of an igneous rock is largely subjective and should be taken only as a very rough guide.

As for minerals, lookalikes are suggested since some rocks can look similar, and this will aid identification. The text for each igneous rock provides additional information, usually with examples of European locations which can be cross-referenced through a trip to the library, or through other resources.

Metamorphic Rocks

There are four main groups of metamorphic rocks, all of which have undergone change. Regional metamorphic rocks may extend for hundreds of kilometres, and are formed from pre-existing rocks (igneous, metamorphic or sedimentary) in response to, for example, major Earth movements, or collision of crustal tectonic plates, as associated with mountain-building. Contact metamorphic rocks form as a result of the high heat around large cooling igneous bodies and may extend for a few kilometres. Cataclastic rocks are mechanically crushed and powdered rocks formed by extreme deformation. Shock metamorphic rocks are produced by crater-forming impacts (*see* Extraterrestrial rocks). Chemical changes may include recrystallisation, replacement of minerals or gains or losses of chemical components during invasion by reactive fluids.

The content of entries for metamorphic rocks is broadly similar to that for igneous rocks as above except for the following.

The chemical grouping is generally more variable, reflecting wider acceptable limits for the minerals making up the named rock; **typical minerals** is less specific than 'essential minerals'.

The **grain size** and texture are generally more significant for identification of metamorphic rocks than proportions of minerals. An additional textural observation, **foliation**, qualitatively describes how strongly aligned mineral bands or grain size variations may be aligned causing planes of weakness across hand specimens and metamorphic rocks in outcrop.

The **conditions** refer to the general pressure (P) -temperature (T) conditions for formation of the rock. As examples, high grade metamorphic rocks from the lower crust, like granulite, have generally experienced the highest P-T conditions with temperatures near 3 GPa, 700°C, at which point the rock may begin to melt (anatexis; *see* migmatite, p.208). Contact metamorphic rocks, like hornfels, generally have minerals which attest to their high-T low-P (<1 GPa) formation. The low temperature boundary where metamorphism begins and diagenesis of sedimentary rocks ends (*see* below) is around 200–300°C. Shock metamorphism in rocks like suevite extends to tremendously high pressures (10–100 GPa).

Sedimentary Rocks

Sedimentary rocks are extremely varied; they cover about 70% of the Earth's surface. Major sedimentary layers can form slowly over very long periods of time, perhaps millions of years. Chemical classifications are more variable, and the Family indicates the general class and chemical affinity of sedimentary rock. Once transported by water, wind or gravity, and deposited, sediments undergo diagenesis, and compaction, involving physical, chemical and biological processes which transform loose sediments into sedimentary rock. There are four main groups: clastic or siliciclastic sediments consist of fragments of pre-existing rocks transported and deposited by physical processes; biogenic sediments are largely of biological and organic origin like limestone; chemical sediments form as precipitates from solution and include evaporites and ironstones; volcaniclastic sediments usually combine siliciclastic materials with contemporaneous products of volcanic activity.

The entries for sedimentary rocks are similar in many respects to both igneous and metamorphic rocks, but with important differences. In addition to minerals, **typical components** may include older rock (lithic) fragments, and fossil debris. Their **material proportions** can vary more widely than for igneous or metamorphic rocks. Physical sediments often show signs of sorting and grain size is an important criterion for classification; with increasing grain size, fine-grained clay (<0.004 mm) grades up into silt (<0.062 mm) and then sand (<2 mm); coarse grain terminology is summarised under the entry for breccia (p.216). Textural features describe both characteristics of hand specimens, and also of the larger scale sedimentary rock exposed as an outcrop. Most sedimentary rocks show subparallel lines representing discrete accumulations known as bedding. Sorting by sedimentation often produces graded bedding with coarse grains at the base, finer grains concentrated upwards. The text entry may list typical locations and also geological eras where the sedimentary rock is well represented in Europe.

Extraterrestrial Rocks

Listed under this category are true extraterrestrials, the meteorites, and also rare shock metamorphic rocks created during formation of impact craters. There are three main families of meteorites, all of which are rare; irons, stony irons and stony meteorites, each with distinctive essential mineral content and textural features. Most meteorite specimens have a dark fusion crust at their edge where they were melted or vaporised by frictional heating during their brief passage through the Earth's atmosphere. The rarest meteorite is believed to have been blasted from the surface of Mars; it is a true Martian rock and has been thought to contain evidence of fossils implying that there has been life on Mars.

Three shock metamorphic rocks are presented to illustrate the products of large impacts on the Earth's crust. Impactite is a melt rock formed near the base of an impact crater when energy from impact is transferred as heat into the target rock. Tektite is a drop of impact melt jetted at high velocity from the impact site, which quenches to a streamlined glass in air and is deposited hundreds or thousands of kilometres away. Suevite is a breccia formed as a chaotic mixture of cold and hot rock particles and other rock fragments within or close to the crater itself. Some relic minerals (eg stishovite: *see* quartz, p.124) within suevites record evidence of the highest known shock pressures on Earth.

WHAT NEXT?

Readers who find they need more information about minerals and rocks, or particular locations, or who would like to contact others with similar interests are encouraged to contact any of the following organisations. If you would like to see a premium collection of minerals and rocks first hand, including fabulous gems, and meteorites, then the Natural History Museum in London (*see* below) offers an outstanding world-class opportunity; they also offer a friendly and expert identification service for those particularly special specimens you may one day discover.

The Mineralogical Society is for both professional and amateur mineralogists. They support a number of special interest groups through meetings and publications. Their resource centre is located in the University of Kingston upon Thames, 41 Queen's Gate, London SW7 5HR Tel: 020 7584 7516 Fax: 020 7823 8021 Website: http://www.minersoc.org/

The Geological Society is for both professional and amateur geologists. They support a number of special interest groups through meetings and publications. Their famous library, accessible to members, is located in central London at Burlington House, Piccadilly, London W1V 0JU Tel: 020 7434 9944 Fax: 020 7439 8975 Website: http://www.geolsoc.org.uk/homepage.htm

The Geological Survey. The BGS is the UK's national centre for earth science information. Several locations; address: Kingsley Dunham Centre, Keyworth, Nottingham NG12 5GG Tel: 0115 936 3100 Fax: 0115 936 3200 Website: http://www.bgs.ac.uk/

The Geologists' Association is devoted both to amateur and professional geologists, through the support of regional groups; they publish particularly useful field guides for popular locations and travel destinations throughout Europe. Address: Burlington House, Piccadilly, London, W1V OJU.

The Natural Environmental Research Council for research information, advice and public information; they serve to encourage public understanding of environmental issues and the role of science. Address: Polaris House, North Star Avenue, Swindon, SN2 1EU Tel: 01793 411 500 Fax: 01793 411501 Website: http://www/nerc.ac.uk/

The Natural History Museum houses 68 million specimens, and offers a world-class resource for minerals, rocks, gems and meteorites. A must-see. Address: Cromwell Road, London, SW7 5BD Tel: 020 7942 5000 Website: http://www.nhm.ac.uk/

Many books are available to cover various levels of interest or expertise in the subjects of mineralogy (minerals) and petrology (rocks). Collins publishes the following recommended guides:
Collins Photoguide Rocks, Minerals and Gemstones by W. Schumann, HarperCollins*Publishers*
Collins Ultimate Guide Rocks and Fossils by A. Busbey, R. Coenraads, D. Roots and P. Willis, HarperCollins*Publishers*

FAMILY: ELEMENT

ID FACT FILE

CRYSTAL SYSTEM:
Cubic

COLOUR:
Copper-red

WHERE:
Hydrothermal

ABUNDANCE:
Common

FORM:
Cubic crystals,
often twinned, or
as thin sheets,
threads or
massive

CLEAVAGE:
None

HARDNESS:
2.5–3

SG:
8.9

LUSTRE:
Metallic

TRANSPARENCY:
Opaque

TESTS:
Hackly fracture.
Soft and
malleable

LOOKALIKES:
None

Copper • Cu

Chemical group: Native element

Native copper occurs as a hydrothermal
deposit associated with alteration of igneous
and volcanic rocks, or infiltrating porous
sedimentary rocks. It may occur in a specific
enriched zone associated with a wide variety of
additional copper minerals (oxides, sulphides,
carbonates etc) in low-grade large-volume
igneous 'porphyry' copper deposits. It often
contains minor amounts of other metals such
as silver and bismuth.

FAMILY: ELEMENT

Diamond • C

Chemical group: Native element

ID FACT FILE

CRYSTAL SYSTEM:
Cubic

COLOUR:
White, colourless
or yellow; rarely
other colours

WHERE:
Metamorphic
mantle

ABUNDANCE:
Rare

FORM:
Equant
octahedral
crystals,
sometimes partly
rounded or
etched

CLEAVAGE:
One perfect
cleavage
direction

HARDNESS:
10

SG:
3.52

LUSTRE:
Brilliant
adamantine

TRANSPARENCY:
Transparent

TESTS:
Hardest
known mineral.
High optical
dispersion

LOOKALIKES:
Various synthetic
gems of lower
hardness

Diamond has unique physical properties. It occurs at high pressure in the Earth's mantle in coarse-grained metamorphic rocks such as eclogite and garnet peridotite. Diamonds have been transported periodically to the Earth's surface by deep-sourced igneous volcanic rocks, such as kimberlites and lamproites. They are mined either from these host igneous rocks, or from secondary placer deposits where they have been secondarily concentrated. The black variety of diamond known as *carbonado* is a compact form of naturally sintered diamond aggregate that is of industrial use.

FAMILY: ELEMENT

ID FACT FILE

CRYSTAL SYSTEM:
Cubic

COLOUR:
Yellow (gold)

WHERE:
Hydrothermal
and alluvial

ABUNDANCE:
Rare

FORM:
Rare cubic
crystals, usually
flakes, rounded
masses,
'nuggets' or
strings

CLEAVAGE:
None

HARDNESS:
2.5–3

SG:
12–20

LUSTRE:
Metallic

TRANSPARENCY:
Opaque

TESTS:
Can be cut with a
knife. Very high
density (SG)

LOOKALIKES:
Pyrite cannot be
cut with knife;
chalcopyrite
breaks beneath
knife blade

Gold • Au (impure)

Chemical group: Native element

Native gold is often alloyed with silver; the impurities vary with locality and may also include copper, iron, palladium, rhodium, etc. These affect the colour; red tints result from copper and silver-rich gold is almost white. They also affect the physical properties; note the large variation in density compared with pure elemental gold (SG = 18.7) reflecting substantial variations in impurities. The colour, density and malleability are distinctive. Chiefly exploited from reworked sedimentary placer deposits, the primary formation of gold is often related to hydrothermal veins associated with quartz. Additional associated minerals may include tellurides and sulphides. Gold is a siderophile (iron-loving) element and most of the Earth's gold budget should reside in the core. Gold is also enriched in meteoritic iron.

FAMILY: ELEMENT

ID FACT FILE

CRYSTAL SYSTEM:
Hexagonal

COLOUR:
Metal-grey

WHERE:
Hydrothermal
and metamorphic

ABUNDANCE:
Common

FORM:
Usually massive;
platy crystals or
'scales'

CLEAVAGE:
Easily cleaved

HARDNESS:
1–2

SG:
2–2.3

LUSTRE:
Metallic

TRANSPARENCY:
Opaque

TESTS:
Black streak.
Cold to touch
due to high
thermal
conductivity

LOOKALIKES:
Molybdenite has
greenish-black
streak

Graphite • C

Chemical group: Native element

Graphite is widely distributed as a minor component of metamorphic rocks, including schists and gneisses. It is sometimes concentrated in igneous hydrothermal veins or in contact metamorphic zones. The high purity graphite deposits which were mined at Borrowdale in the Lake District produced values in excess of £3,000 per ton even in the 19th century, entailing armed guards and full body searches!

FAMILY: ELEMENT

ID FACT FILE

CRYSTAL SYSTEM:
Liquid

COLOUR:
Tin-white

WHERE:
Hydrothermal

ABUNDANCE:
Rare

FORM:
Liquid at room
temperature

CLEAVAGE:
None

HARDNESS:
<1

SG:
13.59

LUSTRE:
Metallic

TRANSPARENCY:
Opaque

TESTS:
High density.
Distinctive
metallic liquid

LOOKALIKES:
None

Mercury • Hg

Chemical group: Native element

Native mercury or 'quicksilver' is a silver-white liquid at room temperature that vaporises at 359°C (678°F). It may occur as droplets in cinnabar, as at Almadén/Spain, with which it forms from hot springs by hydrothermal activity. Mercury produces a vapour which is toxic; touch and physical contact should be avoided.

FAMILY: ELEMENT

Silver • Ag (impure)

Chemical group: Native element

ID FACT FILE

CRYSTAL SYSTEM:
Cubic

COLOUR:
White (silver)

WHERE:
Hydrothermal

ABUNDANCE:
Rare

FORM:
Distorted cubic
crystals, string-
like or massive

CLEAVAGE:
None

HARDNESS:
2.5–3

SG:
10.1–11.1

LUSTRE:
Metallic

TRANSPARENCY:
Opaque

TESTS:
Hackly fracture.
Soft and
malleable

LOOKALIKES:
Silver-coloured
sulphides
(arsenopyrite,
marcasite, etc)
are brittle and
much lower
density

Native silver is usually slightly impure, with small amounts of alloyed metals, often including gold, copper, mercury, platinum, bismuth; these additional components have a minor effect on the physical properties. It occurs in hydrothermal veins, often associated with quartz and sulphides including in particular argentite (Ag_2S), and may be secondarily concentrated in sedimentary placer deposits.

FAMILY: ELEMENT

ID FACT FILE

CRYSTAL SYSTEM:
Orthorhombic

COLOUR:
Sulphur-yellow

WHERE:
Igneous

ABUNDANCE:
Common

FORM:
Crystalline with pyramidal terminations; massive or thin surface encrustations

CLEAVAGE:
Reasonable

HARDNESS:
1.5–2.5

SG:
2.07

LUSTRE:
Resinous

TRANSPARENCY:
Transparent to opaque

TESTS:
Low density

LOOKALIKES:
None

Sulphur • S

Chemical group: Native element

Native sulphur is commonly deposited from volcanic gas emitted from active volcanoes; it is found in volcanic craters and in eroded remnants of volcanic structures. It is also formed as a hydrothermal deposit associated with hot springs. The colour and low density are diagnostic. It may contain small amounts of selenium. Its bright yellow colour is distinctive, both in crystals and surface coatings.

FAMILY: SULPHIDE

Arsenopyrite • FeAsS

Chemical group: Sulphide

ID FACT FILE

CRYSTAL SYSTEM:
Orthorhombic

COLOUR:
Silver-white,
tarnishes

WHERE:
Igneous,
hydrothermal and
metamorphic

ABUNDANCE:
Common

FORM:
Prismatic
crystals or
massive

CLEAVAGE:
Good

HARDNESS:
5.5–6

SG:
5.9–6.2

LUSTRE:
Metallic

TRANSPARENCY:
Opaque

TESTS:
Uneven fracture.
Sparks when hit
with steel and
smells distinctly
of garlic

LOOKALIKES:
Silver is
malleable, and
lacks the garlic
smell when
struck.
Arsenopyrite
crystals
distinctive with
cleavage and
common twinning

Arsenopyrite, also known as 'mispickel', is a widespread hydrothermal sulphide often occurring in mixed sulphide veins (as in Cornwall/England) together with tin, copper, cobalt, nickel and especially lead and silver minerals. Native arsenic (As) also sometimes occurs. The hydrothermal veins are formed during the active cooling stages of large plutonic igneous rocks; mineralisation was often developed along faulted contacts with metamorphic country rocks.

ID FACT FILE

CRYSTAL SYSTEM:
Cubic (high temperature); tetragonal (low temperature)

COLOUR:
Copper-red to brown, tarnished

WHERE:
Igneous, hydrothermal

ABUNDANCE:
Common

FORM:
Crystals may show cube or octahedron

CLEAVAGE:
Poor

HARDNESS:
3

SG:
4.9–5.4

LUSTRE:
Metallic

TRANSPARENCY:
Opaque

TESTS:
Conchoidal to uneven fracture

LOOKALIKES:
None

Bornite • Cu_5FeS_4

Chemical group: Sulphide

Bornite is an important copper iron sulphide valued as a copper ore. Its particular red colour when broken on fresh surfaces is distinctive; fresh surfaces develop an iridescent tarnish with blue, green and purple coloured tints called 'peacock ore'. It occurs in pegmatites and hydrothermal veins often with quartz and chalcopyrite. Also dispersed in copper-rich bedded shales of Permian age in Germany.

FAMILY: SULPHIDE

ID FACT FILE

CRYSTAL SYSTEM:
Orthorhombic

COLOUR:
Black or grey;
subtle blue to
green tarnish

WHERE:
Hydrothermal
and metamorphic

ABUNDANCE:
Common

FORM:
Prismatic
crystals; massive
or granular

CLEAVAGE:
Good

HARDNESS:
2.5–3

SG:
5.5–5.8

LUSTRE:
Metallic

TRANSPARENCY:
Opaque

TESTS:
Conchoidal
fracture. Lead-
grey streak.
Crystals often
twinned

LOOKALIKES:
None

Chalcocite • Cu_2S

Chemical group: Sulphide

Chalcocite, or 'copper glance' as it is also
known, is a simple copper sulphide. It usually
occurs as a secondary alteration of original
chalcopyrite or additional primary copper
minerals. It can form in hydrothermal veins (as
in Cornwall/England). It often represents an
important economic copper mineral in the
secondary enriched zone of large porphyry
copper deposits (as in Chuquicamata/Chile).
The photograph shows a cluster of tiny crystals
greatly magnified.

ID FACT FILE

CRYSTAL SYSTEM:
Tetragonal

COLOUR:
Brass-yellow,
often tarnished

WHERE:
Igneous,
hydrothermal and
metamorphic

ABUNDANCE:
Common

FORM:
Crystals may
show tetrahedral
shapes; massive

CLEAVAGE:
Poor

HARDNESS:
3.5–4

SG:
4.1–4.3

LUSTRE:
Metallic

TRANSPARENCY:
Opaque

TESTS:
Conchoidal to
uneven fracture.
Greenish-black
streak

LOOKALIKES:
Tarnish
resembles
bornite, but
broken fresh
colour
diagnostic.
Distinguished
from gold by its
brittle nature
(and much lower
density)

Chalcopyrite • $CuFeS_2$

Chemical group: Sulphide

Chalcopyrite, previously known as 'copper
pyrite', is one of the most important ore
minerals for copper. Its particular brassy
yellow colour when broken on fresh surfaces is
distinctive; these surfaces develop an
iridescent tarnish similar to bornite. It forms
chiefly as hydrothermal veins (as in
Cornwall/England), and as segregations in
igneous rocks; it is also often associated with
various contact metamorphic rocks.

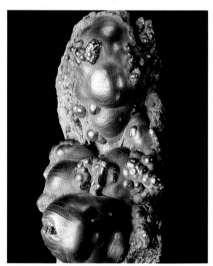

FAMILY: SULPHIDE

Cinnabar • HgS

Chemical group: Sulphide

Cinnabar, mercury sulphide, is formed by hydrothermal activity and hot springs related to volcanism, and is often associated with other sulphide minerals. At the famous locality at Almadén/Spain, it occurs with iron, arsenic and copper sulphides, in a quartzite host rock. Cinnabar has been used as a pigment.

ID FACT FILE

CRYSTAL SYSTEM:
Hexagonal

COLOUR:
Bright vermilion red or brownish red

WHERE:
Igneous and hydrothermal

ABUNDANCE:
Restricted

FORM:
Tabular prismatic crystals; massive or granular

CLEAVAGE:
Good prismatic cleavage

HARDNESS:
2–2.5

SG:
8.1

LUSTRE:
Adamantine or dull

TRANSPARENCY:
Opaque

TESTS:
Commonly associates with mercury

LOOKALIKES:
None

FAMILY: COBALTITE

Cobaltite • CoAsS

Chemical group: Sulphide

The sulpharsenide cobaltite occurs as a primary hydrothermal vein mineral. It often occurs with smaltite and silver, nickel and copper minerals, plus gangue minerals of barite, calcite and quartz, as at Cobalt/Canada. It can contain minor iron impurities. It is an important ore mineral of cobalt.

ID FACT FILE

CRYSTAL SYSTEM:
Cubic

COLOUR:
Silver-white, reddish

WHERE:
Igneous and hydrothermal

ABUNDANCE:
Restricted

FORM:
Cubic crystals; massive or granular

CLEAVAGE:
Poor

HARDNESS:
5.5

SG:
6–6.3

LUSTRE:
Metallic

TRANSPARENCY:
Opaque

TESTS:
Grey-black streak

LOOKALIKES:
None

FAMILY: SULPHIDE

ID FACT FILE

CRYSTAL SYSTEM:
Hexagonal

COLOUR:
Indigo-blue

WHERE:
Hydrothermal

ABUNDANCE:
Common

FORM:
Platy hexagonal crystals; massive

CLEAVAGE:
Distinctive basal cleavage

HARDNESS:
1.5–2

SG:
4.6

LUSTRE:
Metallic

TRANSPARENCY:
Opaque

TESTS:
Very soft, easily scratched with fingernail. Distinctive blue colour

LOOKALIKES:
None

Covellite • CuS

Chemical group: Sulphide

Covellite is a typical secondary copper sulphide mineral developed by relatively low-temperature hydrothermal fluid alteration of primary copper sulphides, such as chalcopyrite. It is an important constituent of secondary enriched layers in large porphyry copper deposits, such as Chuquicamata/Chile. Impurities may include iron and silver.

ID FACT FILE

CRYSTAL SYSTEM:
Monoclinic

COLOUR:
Peach-red or
crimson-red;
rarely greenish

WHERE:
Hydrothermal

ABUNDANCE:
Restricted

FORM:
Earthy,
encrusting of
globular masses;
prismatic
crystals rare

CLEAVAGE:
Perfect

HARDNESS:
1.5–2.5

SG:
3.1

LUSTRE:
Pearly; dull when
massive

TRANSPARENCY:
Transparent to
translucent

TESTS:
Reddish streak.
The streak
powder is
lavender-blue

LOOKALIKES:
Cuprite

FAMILY: VIVIANITE

Erythrite •
$Co_3(AsO_4)_2.8H_2O$

Chemical group: Arsenate

The characteristic colour of erythrite, which
is also known as 'cobalt bloom', makes it a
useful pathfinder to locate cobalt-rich
mineral deposits as at Cobalt, Canada. It
occurs as a secondary oxidation or weathering
product of primary cobalt minerals, such as
cobaltite. Impurities include calcium, nickel
and iron.

FAMILY: SULPHIDE

ID FACT FILE

CRYSTAL SYSTEM:
Cubic

COLOUR:
Lead-grey

WHERE:
Hydrothermal

ABUNDANCE:
Common

FORM:
Cubic crystals;
massive

CLEAVAGE:
Good cleavage
parallel to cube
faces

HARDNESS:
2.5

SG:
7.4–7.6

LUSTRE:
Metallic; dull
tarnish

TRANSPARENCY:
Opaque

TESTS:
Even fracture.
Lead-grey streak

LOOKALIKES:
Antimony
sulphides. The
lead-like colour
of galena
combined with
its propensity to
form cube-
shaped crystals
is diagnostic

Galena • PbS

Chemical group: Sulphide

Galena has been one of the most important ore
minerals for lead since Roman times. It is
formed by hydrothermal fluids often related to
igneous heat sources from cooling plutons.
Galena may contain impurities which are
important in themselves. Thus, 'argentiferous
galena' contains significant amounts of silver;
galena may also contain zinc, iron, copper,
antimony, bismuth and even trace levels of
gold. Selenium may substitute for sulphur. It
frequently occurs together with sphalerite.

FAMILY: COMPLEX SULPHIDE

Jamesonite • $Pb_4FeSb_6S_{14}$

Chemical group: Sulphide

Jamesonite is one of several complex sulphides of antimony (Sb). It is formed by hydrothermal fluids and frequently occurs in veins associated with other antimony-bearing sulphides, and lead-silver- or copper-rich complex antimony-sulphides, as in Cornwall/England.

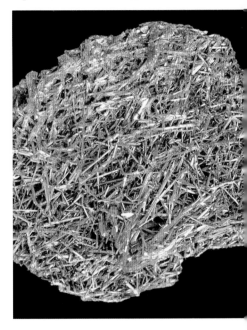

ID FACT FILE

CRYSTAL SYSTEM:
Monoclinic

COLOUR:
Dark lead-grey

WHERE:
Hydrothermal

ABUNDANCE:
Restricted

FORM:
Elongated, acicular crystals, often feathery; massive

CLEAVAGE:
Clear basal cleavage

HARDNESS:
2–3

SG:
5.5–6

LUSTRE:
Metallic

TRANSPARENCY:
Opaque

TESTS:
Dark grey-black streak

LOOKALIKES:
Crystal shapes are distinctive; massive forms are darker grey than galena

FAMILY: IRON ARSENIDE

Löllingite • FeAs$_2$

Chemical group: Arsenide

Löllingite occurs as a primary hydrothermal mineral in mixed sulphide-arsenic vein systems, usually in minor amounts, as in Lölling/Germany. The shiny metallic lustre of fresh broken surfaces contrasts with the dull grey tarnish of weathered surfaces.

ID FACT FILE

CRYSTAL SYSTEM:
Orthorhombic

COLOUR:
Silver-white, tarnishes grey

WHERE:
Hydrothermal

ABUNDANCE:
Restricted

FORM:
Prismatic crystals; disseminated

CLEAVAGE:
Perfect

HARDNESS:
5–5.5

SG:
7.1–7.5

LUSTRE:
Metallic

TRANSPARENCY:
Opaque

TESTS:
Uneven, brittle fracture. Grey-black streak

LOOKALIKES:
Arsenopyrite

ID FACT FILE

CRYSTAL SYSTEM:
Orthorhombic

COLOUR:
Pale bronze-yellow to almost white

WHERE:
Hydrothermal

ABUNDANCE:
Common

FORM:
Crystals commonly tabular and twinned giving cockscomb and spear-shaped groups; also radiating aggregates

CLEAVAGE:
Good

HARDNESS:
6–6.5

SG:
4.9

LUSTRE:
Metallic

TRANSPARENCY:
Opaque

TESTS:
Greyish streak. Uneven fracture, brittle

LOOKALIKES:
It is paler in colour than pyrite

Marcasite • FeS_2

Chemical group: Sulphide

Marcasite is the low-temperature polymorph of pyrite and occurs commonly as a secondary mineral forming concretions in sedimentary rocks where its spherulitic form of radiating crystals is distinctive. It may form by precipitation from low-temperature hydrothermal fluids.

FAMILY: SULPHIDE

ID FACT FILE

CRYSTAL SYSTEM:
Hexagonal

COLOUR:
Lead-grey

WHERE:
Hydrothermal

ABUNDANCE:
Common

FORM:
Usually forms
scales, platy
crystals; or
massive

CLEAVAGE:
Good

HARDNESS:
1–1.5

SG:
4.7–4.8

LUSTRE:
Metallic

TRANSPARENCY:
Opaque

TESTS:
Greenish-grey
streak. Sectile
and almost
malleable

LOOKALIKES:
Greenish streak
distinguishes
molybdenite from
graphite

Molybdenite • MoS$_2$

Chemical group: Sulphide

Small amounts of molybdenite occur in acid
igneous rocks such as granites and granitic
pegmatites. It also occurs in contact
metamorphic zones adjacent to similar granitic
intrusions. Its form of bright grey scaly crystals
is often distinctive and it is further
distinguished by its physical properties
including the ability to be 'flaked' with a
fingernail. May contain selenium.

FAMILY: ARSENIC SULPHIDE

Orpiment • As_2S_3

Chemical group: Sulphide

ID FACT FILE

CRYSTAL SYSTEM:
Monoclinic

COLOUR:
Lemon-yellow,
orange

WHERE:
Igneous,
hydrothermal/
sublimate

ABUNDANCE:
Restricted

FORM:
Rare prismatic
crystals; massive

CLEAVAGE:
Perfect

HARDNESS:
1.5–2

SG:
3.4–3.5

LUSTRE:
Pearly on cleaved
surfaces,
resinous to dull if
massive

TRANSPARENCY:
Translucent

TESTS:
Yellow

LOOKALIKES:
Sulphur

Orpiment is a simple arsenic sulphide formed as a hydrothermal deposit or as a sublimate condensed from hot volcanic gas. It is often associated with realgar, another arsenic sulphide, and with the more oxidised levels of arsenic mineral-rich veins. Its colour and physical properties are diagnostic. It can form an encrusting sublimate from volcanic gas, as at Naples/Italy.

ID FACT FILE

CRYSTAL SYSTEM:
Cubic

COLOUR:
Bronze-yellow

WHERE:
Igneous,
hydrothermal

ABUNDANCE:
Common

FORM:
Usually massive

CLEAVAGE:
Poor

HARDNESS:
3.5–4

SG:
5.0

LUSTRE:
Metallic

TRANSPARENCY:
Opaque

TESTS:
Uneven fracture

LOOKALIKES:
Other sulphides
mainly
distinguished by
colour

Pentlandite • $(Fe,Ni)_9S_8$

Chemical group: Sulphide

Pentlandite is one of the most important economic minerals for nickel. It occurs in association with pyrrhotite in the large nickel deposit at Sudbury/Canada, formed by high-temperature segregation from intrusive igneous rocks. Contains some cobalt.

It oxidises to a variety of secondary nickel minerals, including millerite and niccolite. Pentlandite is also a common secondary mineral in iron meteorites.

FAMILY: PYRITE

ID FACT FILE

CRYSTAL SYSTEM:
Cubic

COLOUR:
Bronze-yellow to pale brass-yellow

WHERE:
Igneous, hydrothermal

ABUNDANCE:
Very common

FORM:
Cube, pyritohedron; often massive

CLEAVAGE:
Cube faces are often strongly striated

HARDNESS:
6–6.5

SG:
4.8–5.1

LUSTRE:
Metallic

TRANSPARENCY:
Opaque

TESTS:
Conchoidal or uneven fracture. Makes sparks when struck with steel. Streak greenish or brownish black

LOOKALIKES:
Chalcopyrite and other sulphides distinguished by physical properties

Pyrite • FeS_2

Chemical group: Sulphide

Pyrite, or 'fools gold', occurs chiefly as a primary mineral in hydrothermal vein systems, and as a low-temperature product in igneous rocks including active volcanic systems. It is widely distributed in all types of rocks as a secondary mineral; it may for example replace fossils in sedimentary rocks. The form and striations on the faces of pyrite crystals are diagnostic. It may contain minor amounts of copper or trace amounts of gold.

FAMILY: SULPHIDE

ID FACT FILE

CRYSTAL SYSTEM:
Hexagonal

COLOUR:
Reddish bronze
or brownish
copper; tarnishes

WHERE:
Igneous,
hydrothermal

ABUNDANCE:
Very common

FORM:
Usually massive;
uncommon
crystals are
hexagonal,
tabular prisms

CLEAVAGE:
May have a good
cleavage

HARDNESS:
3.4–4.5

SG:
4.4–4.7

LUSTRE:
Metallic

TRANSPARENCY:
Opaque

TESTS:
Magnetic.
Conchoidal or
uneven fracture;
brittle. Streak
dark grey-black

LOOKALIKES:
Distinguished
from bornite and
other sulphides
by magnetic and
other physical
properties

Pyrrhotite • FeS

Chemical group: Sulphide

Pyrrhotite is an iron sulphide that often
contains some nickel (up to about 5 per cent),
for which it is exploited. In the largest known
nickel deposit at Sudbury/Canada, it forms
huge ore-bodies together with pentlandite; it
probably formed as magmatic segregations
from an igneous norite and also involved
some hydrothermal activity. It is also found in
typical hydrothermal vein deposits as in
Cornwall/England and Norway. The
photograph shows rare crystals.

FAMILY: SULPHIDE

ID FACT FILE

CRYSTAL SYSTEM:
Monoclinic

COLOUR:
Red to orange

WHERE:
Igneous,
hydrothermal/
sublimate

ABUNDANCE:
Restricted

FORM:
Rare prismatic
crystals;
massive,
granular

CLEAVAGE:
Poor

HARDNESS:
2

SG:
4.5–4.6

LUSTRE:
Resinous

TRANSPARENCY:
Translucent

TESTS:
Red-orange
streak

LOOKALIKES:
None

Realgar • As_2S_2

Chemical group: Sulphide

Realgar is simple arsenic sulphide formed as a
hydrothermal deposit or as a sublimate
condensed from hot volcanic gas. It is often
associated with orpiment, another arsenic
sulphide, or with cinnabar as in Spain. Its
colour and physical properties are diagnostic.
Native arsenic (SG = 5.7) also very occasionally
occurs, and is recognised by its brittle fracture,
steel-grey colour and brilliant lustre.

FAMILY: SPHALERITE

Sphalerite • ZnS

Chemical group: Sulphide

ID FACT FILE

CRYSTAL SYSTEM:
Cubic

COLOUR:
Yellowish brown or black; occasionally yellow or white

WHERE:
Igneous, hydrothermal

ABUNDANCE:
Very common

FORM:
Crystals usually tetrahedra or rhombododeca-hedra; massive

CLEAVAGE:
Good

HARDNESS:
3.5–4

SG:
3.9–4.2

LUSTRE:
Resinous to adamantine

TRANSPARENCY:
Translucent to transparent

TESTS:
Conchoidal fracture; brittle. Streak white to yellow and brown

LOOKALIKES:
None

Sphalerite is probably the most common zinc mineral and forms in hydrothermal vein systems of various types often with galena and other sulphides, as for example in Cornwall and Derbyshire. Almost all sphalerite contains some iron; other impurities may include arsenic, mercury, iron and cadmium.

ID FACT FILE

CRYSTAL SYSTEM:
Tetragonal

COLOUR:
Grey to bronze or yellowish; tarnishes

WHERE:
Hydrothermal

ABUNDANCE:
Restricted

FORM:
Usually massive, granular; rare crystals

CLEAVAGE:
Poor

HARDNESS:
4

SG:
4.4

LUSTRE:
Metallic

TRANSPARENCY:
Opaque

TESTS:
Blackish streak

LOOKALIKES:
Cassiterite

Stannite • Cu_2FeSnS_4

Chemical group: Sulphide

Stannite is a complex sulphide of tin, copper and iron and often contains minor zinc in addition. It is an important source of tin, and often occurs in hydrothermal deposits with cassiterite and other iron, copper, silver and arsenic minerals. It may also contain traces of germanium.

FAMILY: ANTIMONY SULPHIDE

Stibnite • Sb_2S_3

Chemical group: Sulphide

ID FACT FILE

CRYSTAL SYSTEM:
Orthorhombic

COLOUR:
Lead-grey

WHERE:
Hydrothermal

ABUNDANCE:
Restricted

FORM:
Elongated
crystals, bladed,
sheaves; crystals
may be curved

CLEAVAGE:
Good

HARDNESS:
2

SG:
4.5–4.6

LUSTRE:
Metallic

TRANSPARENCY:
Opaque

TESTS:
Lead-grey streak.
Lower density
than galena.
Subconchoidal or
brittle fracture

LOOKALIKES:
Crystal shapes
are distinctive;
massive forms
are darker grey
than galena

Stibnite is the simple trisulphide of antimony
(Sb). It is formed by hydrothermal fluids
and frequently occurs in quartz-stibnite veins
but also occurs with quartz, dolomite, calcite
and barite in 'white' veins as in Cornwall/
England. Antimony rarely occurs as the native
element, and stibnite is perhaps the most
important economic primary mineral of
antimony.

Tennantite • $(Cu,Fe)_{12}As_4S_{13}$

Chemical group: Arsenic-sulphide

ID FACT FILE

CRYSTAL SYSTEM:
Cubic

COLOUR:
Grey with olive tint

WHERE:
Hydrothermal

ABUNDANCE:
Restricted

FORM:
Well-shaped crystals (tetrahedra); granular or dense aggregates

CLEAVAGE:
None

HARDNESS:
3–4.5

SG:
4.6–4.8

LUSTRE:
Metallic-dull

TRANSPARENCY:
Opaque; very thin splinters are reddish

TESTS:
Conchoidal brittle fracture. Black to reddish brown streak

LOOKALIKES:
Tetrahedrite

Usually occurs as a massive or encrusting dark grey mineral. Well-formed crystals may show distinctive triangular faces (tetrahedral faces) similar in many respects to tetrahedrite (*see* p.42). It is found in copper and lead bearing hydrothermal vein systems, associated with tetrahedrite, siderite, galena and sphalerite, as in Cornwall/England), Harz/Saxony/Germany, Boliden/Sweden, Alsace/France.

FAMILY: TETRAHEDRITE

Tetrahedrite • $(Cu,Fe)_{12}Sb_4S_{13}$

Chemical group: Antimony-sulphide

ID FACT FILE

CRYSTAL SYSTEM:
Cubic

COLOUR:
Grey with olive tint

WHERE:
Hydrothermal

ABUNDANCE:
Restricted

FORM:
Well-shaped crystals (tetrahedra); granular or dense aggregates

CLEAVAGE:
None

HARDNESS:
3–4

SG:
4.6–5.2

LUSTRE:
Metallic-dull

TRANSPARENCY:
Opaque; very thin splinters are reddish

TESTS:
Conchoidal brittle fracture. Black to brown streak

LOOKALIKES:
Tennantite

Tetrahedrite occurs in copper- and lead-bearing hydrothermal vein systems, associated with siderite, galena and sphalerite, as in Cornwall/England and Harz/Germany. Impurities are often economically important and can include iron, silver, zinc, gold or mercury. Crystals are usually very distinctive with four triangular faces (tetrahedra), sometimes twinned.

FAMILY: FLUORIDE

Fluorite • CaF$_2$

Chemical group: Halide

ID FACT FILE

CRYSTAL SYSTEM:
Cubic

COLOUR:
Variable;
colourless,
white, green,
purple, blue or
yellow

WHERE:
Hydrothermal,
igneous

ABUNDANCE:
Common

FORM:
Common cube
crystals, rarely
other shapes;
also granular

CLEAVAGE:
Perfect
(octahedral)

HARDNESS:
4

SG:
3–3.25

LUSTRE:
Vitreous

TRANSPARENCY:
Transparent to
translucent

TESTS:
Conchoidal to
uneven fracture;
brittle. Crystals
may be
concentrically
zoned in colour

LOOKALIKES:
Coloured fluorite
'cubes' are
unlikely to be
mistaken

Fluorite is formed by hydrothermal fluids and usually occurs in vein systems related to large igneous bodies; it is often associated with sphalerite, galena, barite and quartz, as in the Pennines/England. It can also occur as a primary mineral in some alkaline igneous rocks, such as syenite pegmatites and carbonatites. Displays a wide variety of colours and may be zoned; very distinctive cubes.

FAMILY: CHLORIDE

Halite • NaCl

Chemical group: Halide

ID FACT FILE

CRYSTAL SYSTEM:
Cubic

COLOUR:
Colourless, white, yellow, red

WHERE:
Sedimentary

ABUNDANCE:
Abundant

FORM:
Common cube crystals; also massive

CLEAVAGE:
Perfect

HARDNESS:
2–2.5

SG:
2.2

LUSTRE:
Vitreous

TRANSPARENCY:
Transparent to translucent

TESTS:
Tastes saline (test not recommended). Soluble in water

LOOKALIKES:
Sylvite, KCl, tastes more bitter and crystals can show octahedral faces

Halite forms by evaporation of saline bodies of water, such as sabkhas. Substantial bedded deposits of 'rock salt' occur throughout the stratigraphic record, including within the Permian in Germany, and within the Trias in Cheshire. Halite can occur with a variety of additional evaporite minerals, such as complex sulphates and carbonates of calcium, magnesium and potassium; sylvite, KCl, is the potassium equivalent of halite.

FAMILY: CHLORIDE

ID FACT FILE

CRYSTAL SYSTEM:
Cubic

COLOUR:
Colourless or white

WHERE:
Sedimentary, volcanic

ABUNDANCE:
Abundant

FORM:
Common cube crystals; also granular

CLEAVAGE:
Perfect

HARDNESS:
1.5–2

SG:
2.0

LUSTRE:
Vitreous, greasy

TRANSPARENCY:
Transparent to translucent

TESTS:
Uneven, brittle fracture. Tastes bitter (test not recommended). Soluble in water

LOOKALIKES:
Halite. KCl tastes more bitter and crystals can show octahedral faces

Sylvite • KCl

Chemical group: Halide

Sylvite occurs in evaporite and potash salt deposits. It is usually associated with halite and other chlorides (*see* halite p.44). Sylvite tastes more bitter than halite and crystals may have small additional corner faces (triangular). Tends to be hygroscopic (attracts water) and softer than halite. Also occurs as volcanic sublimate, as at Mt Vesuvius/Italy. Common constituent of desiccating hyperalkaline lakes, as in Chilean Andes at Calama.

FAMILY: TIN OXIDE

ID FACT FILE

CRYSTAL SYSTEM:
Tetragonal

COLOUR:
Black, brown, yellow or reddish

WHERE:
Hydrothermal, igneous, placers

ABUNDANCE:
Common

FORM:
Squat terminated prisms; also fibrous or massive

CLEAVAGE:
Reasonable

HARDNESS:
7

SG:
6.6–7.1

LUSTRE:
Adamantine, greasy

TRANSPARENCY:
Transparent to opaque

TESTS:
Conchoidal, brittle. White, brownish streak

LOOKALIKES:
Zircon

Cassiterite • SnO_2

Chemical group: Oxide

Cassiterite (*tinstone*) occurs in hydrothermal vein systems often with abundant quartz associated with boron or fluorine minerals (fluorite, tourmaline, axinite, etc). It also occurs in granite pegmatites and in metasomatised granites called 'greisens' or adjacent metamorphosed country rocks. Cassiterite occurs in secondary placer deposits, which are often of economic value. Formerly an important ore mineral for the tin industry.

FAMILY: HEMATITE

Corundum • Al_2O_3

Chemical group: Oxide

ID FACT FILE

CRYSTAL SYSTEM:
Hexagonal

COLOUR:
Grey, green, red, blue, yellow

WHERE:
Igneous, metamorphic, placers

ABUNDANCE:
Common

FORM:
Barrel-shaped or pointed prisms; also fibrous or massive

CLEAVAGE:
None

HARDNESS:
9

SG:
4–4.1

LUSTRE:
Vitreous

TRANSPARENCY:
Transparent to opaque

TESTS:
Conchoidal, splintery, brittle. White streak

LOOKALIKES:
Hardness is unlikely to be mistaken

Corundum occurs as a primary mineral in igneous and metamorphic rocks. It is the second hardest mineral known. Common varieties are cloudy. Clear varieties are used to make gemstones. *Ruby* is red and occurs in marble, schist and placer deposits. *Sapphire* refers to all coloured gem varieties which are not red, including pink, blue or yellow varieties, and occurs in contact metamorphic rocks, in placers and in some igneous rocks, as in Thailand and Montana/USA.

FAMILY: COPPER OXIDE

ID FACT FILE

CRYSTAL SYSTEM:
Cubic

COLOUR:
Red shades

WHERE:
Hydrothermal

ABUNDANCE:
Restricted

FORM:
Crystals often
small octahedra;
also massive,
granular

CLEAVAGE:
Perfect

HARDNESS:
3.5–4

SG:
5.8–6.2

LUSTRE:
Metallic, dull

TRANSPARENCY:
Translucent to
opaque

TESTS:
Conchoidal,
uneven, brittle.
Brown-red streak

LOOKALIKES:
Crocoite,
limonite

Cuprite • Cu_2O

Chemical group: Oxide

Cuprite, simple copper oxide, is a typical
secondary copper mineral formed in the
oxidised zones of hydrothermal and porphyry
copper deposits. It often forms from the
breakdown of primary sulphides of copper; it
may be associated with native copper, and iron
oxides such as limonite.

ID FACT FILE

CRYSTAL SYSTEM:
Orthorhombic

COLOUR:
Colourless, white

WHERE:
Sedimentary, metamorphic

ABUNDANCE:
Abundant

FORM:
Small tabular crystals rare; lamellar aggregates, massive

CLEAVAGE:
Perfect

HARDNESS:
6.5–7

SG:
3.3–3.5

LUSTRE:
Vitreous to pearly

TRANSPARENCY:
Transparent to translucent

TESTS:
Conchoidal, brittle. White streak

LOOKALIKES:
Mixed Al-hydroxides in bauxite

Diaspore • AlOOH

Chemical group: Hydroxide

Diaspore occurs with other hydroxides of aluminium, such as gibbsite, in the red-brown tropical weathering product of silicate rocks called bauxite. *Bauxite* is an important economic ore for aluminium, as in Brazil. Diaspore is also a secondary mineral with corundum in metamorphic rocks.

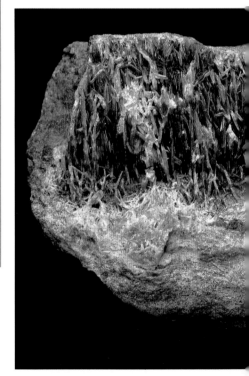

FAMILY: IRON OXIDE

Hematite • Fe_2O_3

Chemical group: Oxide

ID FACT FILE

CRYSTAL SYSTEM:
Hexagonal-trigonal

COLOUR:
Black, grey, red-brown

WHERE:
Igneous, sedimentary, metamorphic

ABUNDANCE:
Abundant

FORM:
Chunky to platy crystals; granular, radiating and globular

CLEAVAGE:
None

HARDNESS:
6–6.5

SG:
4.9–5.3

LUSTRE:
Metallic, dull

TRANSPARENCY:
Opaque except very thin flakes blood-red

TESTS:
Conchoidal, brittle. Cherry-red streak

LOOKALIKES:
Pyrolusite, psilomelane

Hematite occurs widely in a variety of forms in many different rocks. 'Kidney ore' is massive with a distinctive smooth globular surface and internal radiating structure. 'Specular iron' consists of abundant shiny metallic hematite crystals. 'Reddle' is earthy hematite used as a pigment and a polish. 'Micaceous iron' is thin lamellar hematite crystals. An important ore mineral for iron, it has been mined in Cumberland/England, Elba/Italy, Bilbao/Spain and many other countries.

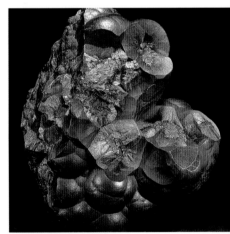

FAMILY: IRON TITANIUM OXIDE

ID FACT FILE

CRYSTAL SYSTEM:
Trigonal

COLOUR:
Black tinted
violet

WHERE:
Igneous,
sedimentary

ABUNDANCE:
Common

FORM:
Tabular to platy
crystals; granular
aggregates or
dispersed

CLEAVAGE:
None

HARDNESS:
5–6

SG:
4.5–5

LUSTRE:
Metallic, dull

TRANSPARENCY:
Opaque

TESTS:
Conchoidal,
brittle. Brown-
black streak

LOOKALIKES:
Iron oxides

Ilmenite • $FeTiO_3$

Chemical group: Oxide

Ilmenite occurs widely in small quantities in
igneous rocks like gabbros; sometimes large
accumulations are important for titanium and
have been mined in Norway and Sweden. It is
more resistant to weathering than pure iron
oxides and can form economic deposits in
beach sands, as in India and Australia.
Impurities can include magnesia and
admixtures of other iron oxides, with which it is
often associated.

FAMILY: SPINEL

Magnetite • Fe_3O_4

Chemical group: Oxide

ID FACT FILE

CRYSTAL SYSTEM:
Cubic

COLOUR:
Black

WHERE:
Igneous,
sedimentary,
metamorphic

ABUNDANCE:
Abundant

FORM:
Equant well-
formed crystals;
granular
aggregates

CLEAVAGE:
Imperfect

HARDNESS:
5.5

SG:
5.2

LUSTRE:
Metallic, dull

TRANSPARENCY:
Opaque

TESTS:
Conchoidal,
brittle. Black
streak. Strongly
magnetic

LOOKALIKES:
Iron oxides,
chromite

Magnetite occurs in small quantities in most igneous rocks; sometimes large accumulations are economic as in Sweden, Finland and the Urals. It also occurs in metamorphic skarn, in schist and in 'black sand' placer deposits. Impurities include magnesia and titanium. It is the most widespread economic ore of iron. Strong crystal shapes (octahedra) even for very small crystals, are typical. Magnetic properties cause a compass needle to swing. Variety titanomagnetite contains titanium. Photograph shows magnetic properties with sticking pins.

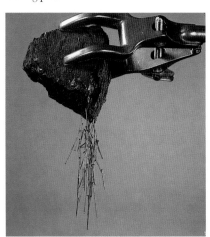

ID FACT FILE

CRYSTAL SYSTEM:
Orthorhombic

COLOUR:
Brown, black, occasionally yellow

WHERE:
Igneous

ABUNDANCE:
Common

FORM:
Stubby crystals, prismatic; granular dispersed

CLEAVAGE:
Good

HARDNESS:
5.5

SG:
4.0–4.8

LUSTRE:
Metallic, greasy

TRANSPARENCY:
Transparent to opaque

TESTS:
Conchoidal, brittle fracture. White streak

LOOKALIKES:
Spinel, pyrochlore, melanite

Perovskite • CaTiO$_3$

Chemical group: Titanate

Perovskite is a common accessory mineral in alkaline igneous rocks, including nephelinite, ijolite, pegmatite and carbonatite. Impurities include rare earth elements, zirconium and niobium. Usually forms small granular crystals distinguished from otherwise similar pyrochlore by streak test. Perovskite is also stable at high pressure and usually present in small amounts in igneous rocks from greatest depth such as kimberlite. A synthetic magnesium silicate variety of perovskite with similar structure is thought to be the most abundant mineral in the Earth's lower mantle.

FAMILY: PYROCHLORE

ID FACT FILE

CRYSTAL SYSTEM:
Cubic

COLOUR:
Brown, black,
occasionally
yellow

WHERE:
Igneous

ABUNDANCE:
Common

FORM:
Good crystals,
cubes, or 8-sided
(octahedra);
massive

CLEAVAGE:
None

HARDNESS:
5–5.5

SG:
3.5–4.6

LUSTRE:
Adamantine,
greasy

TRANSPARENCY:
Opaque to
translucent

TESTS:
Conchoidal,
uneven, brittle
fracture. Yellow-
brown streak

LOOKALIKES:
Spinel, melanite

Pyrochlore • $(Na,Ca)_2$ $(Nb,Ta)_2O_6(O,OH,F)$

Chemical group: Oxide

Pyrochlore is a common accessory mineral in
alkaline igneous rocks, including pegmatites
and carbonatites. Impurities include rare
earth elements, uranium and thorium.
Niobium-rich varieties may be pale-coloured
or yellow. The niobium is often partly
replaced by tantalum; the pure tantalum
variety is called microlite. Forms economic
deposits for niobium and tantalum
concentrated by weathering of carbonatites,
as in Brazil and East Africa.

FAMILY: MANGANESE DIOXIDE

ID FACT FILE

CRYSTAL SYSTEM:
Tetragonal

COLOUR:
Black, grey

WHERE:
Sedimentary, hydrothermal

ABUNDANCE:
Common

FORM:
Massive, globular or radiating; small crystals rare

CLEAVAGE:
Perfect

HARDNESS:
Crystals 6.5, massive 2–6

SG:
4.7

LUSTRE:
Metallic, dull

TRANSPARENCY:
Opaque

TESTS:
Uneven, brittle fracture. Black streak. Often slightly stains hands

LOOKALIKES:
Hematite, romanechite

Pyrolusite • MnO_2

Chemical group: Oxide

Pyrolusite is a chief source of manganese and occurs in sedimentary rocks either as precipitates with iron, or by weathering and replacing of manganese-bearing minerals, typically silicates. This can result in aggregates, nodules and layers with clays, such as laterites in Brazil and India. The photograph shows rare small crystals (enlarged).

FAMILY: PSILOMELANE

ID FACT FILE

CRYSTAL SYSTEM:
Monoclinic

COLOUR:
Black, grey

WHERE:
Hydrothermal

ABUNDANCE:
Restricted

FORM:
Massive,
globular or
stalactitic;
crystals unknown

CLEAVAGE:
None

HARDNESS:
5–6

SG:
4.7

LUSTRE:
Metallic, dull

TRANSPARENCY:
Opaque

TESTS:
Uneven, brittle
fracture. Black-
brown streak

LOOKALIKES:
Hematite,
pyrolusite

Romanechite • $(Ba, H_2O)_2Mn_5O_{10}$

Chemical group: Oxide

Romanechite (previously called psilomelane) is one of several manganese oxides belonging to the psilomelane group, which are manganese oxide minerals containing some structural water (hydrous). It occurs as a secondary mineral in the oxidation zone of hydrothermal manganese ore deposits. Often associated with pyrolusite, as in Cornwall/England, Saxony and Black Forest/Germany. Impurities may include some iron and potassium.

FAMILY: TITANIUM OXIDE

Rutile • TiO$_2$

Chemical group: Oxide

ID FACT FILE

CRYSTAL SYSTEM:
Tetragonal

COLOUR:
Red, brown, yellow, black

WHERE:
Igneous, metamorphic

ABUNDANCE:
Common

FORM:
Elongated crystals, needles or twinned larger crystals; massive granular

CLEAVAGE:
Poor

HARDNESS:
6–6.5

SG:
4.2

LUSTRE:
Adamantine, metallic

TRANSPARENCY:
Transparent to opaque

TESTS:
Conchoidal, uneven, brittle fracture. Yellowish-brown streak

LOOKALIKES:
None

Rutile is the simple oxide of titanium and is an important source of titanium. It is a widespread minor constituent of igneous rocks such as granites, diorites and pegmatites. It also occurs in metamorphic gneisses and amphibolites. May be concentrated by secondary weathering into economic beach sand deposits as in Australia, South Africa and Florida/USA. It also occurs as fine fibrous needles distributed through quartz crystals called 'rutilated quartz'. The photograph shows a small well-formed crystal much enlarged.

FAMILY: SPINEL

Spinel • MgAl₂O₄

Chemical group: Oxide

Spinel is one member of a family of spinels
with large ranges in composition; most spinel
contains some chromium, iron and manganese.
It occurs in igneous rocks like basalt, gabbro
and peridotite, and in metamorphic rocks like
schists, hornfels and marble. Coloured
varieties (especially blue and red) used for
gems occur in placer deposits as in Thailand
and Burma. Varieties include black-coloured
hercynite ($FeAl_2O_4$), and *chromite* ($FeCr_2O_4$).
Igneous chromite concentrations are mined for
chromium, as in South Africa.

ID FACT FILE

CRYSTAL SYSTEM:
Cubic

COLOUR:
All colours,
commonly red,
black, brown

WHERE:
Igneous,
metamorphic

ABUNDANCE:
Common

FORM:
Well-formed
crystals
(octahedra)

CLEAVAGE:
Imperfect

HARDNESS:
8

SG:
3.5–4.1

LUSTRE:
Vitreous

TRANSPARENCY:
Transparent to
opaque

TESTS:
Conchoidal,
brittle fracture.
White streak

LOOKALIKES:
Garnet,
pyrochlore

FAMILY: URANIUM OXIDE

Uraninite • UO_2

Chemical group: Oxide

ID FACT FILE

CRYSTAL SYSTEM:
Cubic

COLOUR:
Black

WHERE:
Igneous,
hydrothermal

ABUNDANCE:
Uncommon

FORM:
Crystals small
cubes or
octahedra; also
massive

CLEAVAGE:
None

HARDNESS:
4–6

SG:
9.1–10.6

LUSTRE:
Greasy, dull

TRANSPARENCY:
Opaque

TESTS:
Conchoidal,
uneven fracture.
Black, greenish
streak. Strongly
radioactive

LOOKALIKES:
Radioactivity and
high density
unlikely to be
mistaken

Uraninite (old name 'pitchblende') is often impure, containing some thorium, zirconium and lead. It occurs as a primary mineral in igneous rocks like granites and pegmatites; also in hydrothermal vein systems with lead, copper and tin minerals as in Cornwall/ England, Saxony/Germany and the Congo. It is an important source of uranium. In addition to the normal physical tests, uraninite is strongly radioactive; it can be detected with a geiger counter and is a serious health hazard.

FAMILY: APATITE

Vanadinite • $Pb_5(VO_4)_3Cl$

Chemical group: Vanadate

ID FACT FILE

CRYSTAL SYSTEM:
Hexagonal

COLOUR:
Ruby-red, orange-brown or yellowish

WHERE:
Hydrothermal

ABUNDANCE:
Restricted

FORM:
Stubby prismatic crystals; sometimes encrusting

CLEAVAGE:
None

HARDNESS:
3

SG:
6.5–7.1

LUSTRE:
Adamantine, greasy

TRANSPARENCY:
Opaque

TESTS:
Conchoidal, brittle fracture. Pale yellow streak

LOOKALIKES:
Pyromorphite, crocoite, cuprite

Vanadinite is a lead vanadate mineral usually with a distinctive bright reddish colour. It often contains some phosphorous and arsenic. It occurs as a secondary mineral in the oxidation zone of hydrothermal lead vein systems, as in Namibia, Zambia and Arizona/USA. Often associated with other oxidised lead minerals such as pyromorphite; it is sometimes an economic source of vanadium. The photograph shows clusters of small crystals much enlarged.

FAMILY: WOLFRAMITE

Wolframite •
(Fe,Mn)WO$_4$

Chemical group: Tungstate

ID FACT FILE

CRYSTAL SYSTEM:
Monoclinic

COLOUR:
Brown-black

WHERE:
Hydrothermal

ABUNDANCE:
Restricted

FORM:
Tabular crystals, bladed or massive

CLEAVAGE:
Perfect

HARDNESS:
5–5.5

SG:
7.1–7.6

LUSTRE:
Metallic to dull

TRANSPARENCY:
Transparent to opaque

TESTS:
Uneven fracture. Chocolate-brown streak

LOOKALIKES:
Ilmenite

Wolframite is a simple iron tungstate with some additional manganese. It occurs in hydrothermal vein systems associated with tin minerals and quartz as in Cornwall/England and Bolivia. It is the most important ore mineral for tungsten (W). The precise amount of iron and manganese varies considerably, and it may contain some calcium. Wolframite derived from tungsten-tin veins also forms economic sedimentary placer deposits, as in Burma.

FAMILY: CARBONATE

ID FACT FILE

CRYSTAL SYSTEM:
Hexagonal

COLOUR:
Brown

WHERE:
Sedimentary,
igneous

ABUNDANCE:
Uncommon

FORM:
Well-shaped
(rhombohedral)
crystals, often
with curved
faces; also
massive or
granular

CLEAVAGE:
Perfect
(rhombohedral)

HARDNESS:
3.5–4

SG:
4

LUSTRE:
Crystals vitreous
to pearly;
massive dull

TRANSPARENCY:
Translucent to
opaque

TESTS:
Conchoidal to
uneven fracture;
brittle. Curved
faces of crystals.
Dissolves slowly
in dilute HCl

LOOKALIKES:
Dolomite is paler

Ankerite •
$Ca(Fe,Mg)(CO_3)_2$

Chemical group: Carbonate

Ankerite is the uncommon iron-rich equivalent
of dolomite. It occurs in sedimentary rocks
modified by iron-rich mineralisation, or where
iron is otherwise abundant. It also occurs as a
primary mineral in rare iron-rich varieties of
igneous carbonate rocks, such as iron-rich
carbonatites. It often forms well-shaped
crystals with slightly curved faces and
resembles a brown-coloured form of dolomite.

FAMILY: CALCIUM CARBONATE

ID FACT FILE

CRYSTAL SYSTEM:
Orthorhombic

COLOUR:
White, yellowish or grey

WHERE:
Sedimentary, hydrothermal

ABUNDANCE:
Abundant

FORM:
Sharp pointed prismatic crystals, often twinned; radiating acicular needles, also corals, stalactites and encrusting forms

CLEAVAGE:
Perfect (rhombohedral)

HARDNESS:
3.5–4

SG:
2.9

LUSTRE:
Vitreous

TRANSPARENCY:
Transparent to translucent

TESTS:
Subconchoidal fracture; brittle. Dissolves easily in dilute HCl

LOOKALIKES:
Calcite is less hard

Aragonite • $CaCO_3$

Chemical group: Carbonate

Aragonite is the high-pressure form (polymorph) of $CaCO_3$ calcite, into which it changes upon heating. Small amounts of lead and strontium may be present. It can occur with sedimentary gypsum deposits, and is also accreted biologically to form the basic structure of many corals. It is slightly harder than calcite where it occurs as prismatic crystals (*see* photograph); these are of a different shape to calcite.

FAMILY: COPPER CARBONATE

Azurite •
$Cu_3(CO_3)_2(OH)_2$

Chemical group: Carbonate

ID FACT FILE

CRYSTAL SYSTEM:
Monoclinic

COLOUR:
Deep blue (azure blue)

WHERE:
Hydrothermal

ABUNDANCE:
Common

FORM:
Prismatic crystals uncommon, sometimes radiating aggregates, often massive

CLEAVAGE:
Good

HARDNESS:
3.5–4

SG:
3.8

LUSTRE:
Vitreous

TRANSPARENCY:
Transparent to opaque

TESTS:
Conchoidal fracture; brittle. Effervesces in dilute HCl. Pale blue streak

LOOKALIKES:
Unlikely to confuse colour and streak

Azurite is a basic hydrated copper carbonate, similar to malachite. It has a distinctive deep azure blue colour and has been used as a pigment. It occurs as a secondary copper mineral in the oxidised zone of hydrothermal veins and porphyry copper deposits, often together with malachite, cuprite and native copper. The photograph shows rare substantial crystals of azurite.

FAMILY: CALCIUM CARBONATE

ID FACT FILE

CRYSTAL SYSTEM:
Hexagonal

COLOUR:
Colourless, white;
sometimes tinted
with other colours

WHERE:
Igneous,
sedimentary,
metamorphic

ABUNDANCE:
Rock-forming

FORM:
Prismatic
crystals of
several varieties,
commonly
twinned; also
occurs nodular,
granular,
stalactitic,
compact, earthy

CLEAVAGE:
Perfect
(rhombohedral)

HARDNESS:
3

SG:
2.71

LUSTRE:
Vitreous to
earthy

TRANSPARENCY:
Transparent to
opaque

TESTS:
Conchoidal but
cleaves easily.
Dissolves in
dilute HCl. White
streak

LOOKALIKES:
Carbonates

Calcite • $CaCO_3$

Chemical group: Carbonate

Calcite is the principal rock-forming mineral of several sedimentary rocks, including limestones and chalk. It forms the shells of many biological organisms. It also occurs as a hydrothermal mineral, as a primary mineral in igneous carbonatite and is widespread in metamorphic rocks. Calcite may be of organic or inorganic origin. It may contain a variety of impurities including iron, magnesium, manganese, lead and strontium. 'Dog tooth spar' (illustrated) and 'Iceland spar' are particularly well-formed crystal varieties of calcite.

FAMILY: LEAD CARBONATE

ID FACT FILE

CRYSTAL SYSTEM:
Orthorhombic

COLOUR:
Colourless, white
or greyish;
sometimes
tinted blue or
green

WHERE:
Hydrothermal

ABUNDANCE:
Restricted

FORM:
Prismatic tabular
crystals; twinning
can give
cruciform or
radiating
aggregates; also
stalactitic,
massive

CLEAVAGE:
Imperfect

HARDNESS:
3–3.5

SG:
6.6

LUSTRE:
Adamantine,
vitreous or
resinous

TRANSPARENCY:
Transparent to
opaque

TESTS:
Conchoidal,
brittle. Dissolves
in dilute HCl.
White streak

LOOKALIKES:
Barite

Cerussite • $PbCO_3$

Chemical group: Carbonate

Cerussite is simple lead carbonate. It occurs in
the weathering zone of lead deposits, and is
often associated with galena and anglesite. It
occurs at most lead mineral localities and is
locally an important lead ore. As for many
carbonate minerals it dissolves in dilute
hydrochloric acid (HCl). High densirty (SG)
can be distinctive.

FAMILY: COMPOUND CARBONATE

ID FACT FILE

CRYSTAL SYSTEM:
Hexagonal

COLOUR:
Colourless, white, pink, greyish or various tints

WHERE:
Igneous, sedimentary, metamorphic

ABUNDANCE:
Rock-forming

FORM:
Prismatic crystals, frequently curved, mostly rhombohedral; also massive, porous or granular

CLEAVAGE:
Perfect

HARDNESS:
3.5–4

SG:
2.9

LUSTRE:
Vitreous

TRANSPARENCY:
Transparent to translucent

TESTS:
Conchoidal fracture, brittle. Dissolves slowly in dilute HCl. White or pale grey streak

LOOKALIKES:
Ankerite

Dolomite • $CaMg(CO_3)_2$

Chemical group: Carbonate

Dolomite is a mixed calcium-magnesium carbonate. It is a rock-forming mineral in sedimentary dolomites, metamorphic marbles, and together with calcite in limestones. It also occurs in hydrothermal mineral veins. Dolomite forms a complete compositional series with ankerite. In addition to iron, impurities may include manganese, strontium and lead. Crystalline forms have distinctive curved crystal edges. Dissolves reluctantly in dilute HCl.

FAMILY: MAGNESIUM CARBONATE

ID FACT FILE

CRYSTAL SYSTEM:
Hexagonal

COLOUR:
White, greyish or brownish; chalky

WHERE:
Hydrothermal

ABUNDANCE:
Restricted

FORM:
Usually massive, fibrous or granular; rare crystals similar to dolomite

CLEAVAGE:
Perfect

HARDNESS:
3.5–4.5

SG:
3

LUSTRE:
Fibrous earthy; crystals vitreous

TRANSPARENCY:
Transparent to opaque

TESTS:
Flat conchoidal fracture. Dissolves slowly in dilute HCl. White streak

LOOKALIKES:
Chalk

Magnesite • $MgCO_3$

Chemical group: Carbonate

Magnesite is a simple magnesium carbonate. It occurs as a secondary replacement vein mineral in ultramafic rocks altered by fluids; it also sometimes forms significant bodies of magnesite-rich rock by metasomatic replacement of original sedimentary dolomite and limestone adjacent to intrusive igneous rocks. Crystalline forms are rare and in its normal massive white form it closely resembles the rock chalk, but is somewhat harder than calcite.

FAMILY: COPPER CARBONATE

Malachite •
$Cu_2CO_3(OH)_2$

Chemical group: Carbonate

ID FACT FILE

CRYSTAL SYSTEM:
Monoclinic

COLOUR:
Bright green, often banded

WHERE:
Hydrothermal

ABUNDANCE:
Common

FORM:
Usually massive, encrusting, stalactitic with smooth botryoidal surface; internally fibrous, compact or earthy

CLEAVAGE:
Perfect

HARDNESS:
3.5–4

SG:
3.9

LUSTRE:
Silky to earthy

TRANSPARENCY:
Translucent (crystals) to opaque

TESTS:
Flat conchoidal fracture. Green streak

LOOKALIKES:
Chrysocolla

The attractive green colours of malachite are distinctive, and it is often polished as an ornament. It is perhaps the best known copper carbonate mineral. Its bright green colours have been used as a pigment. The colour banding represents successive growth from hydrothermal fluids, in veins and in the oxidised zone of copper deposits. It often occurs with azurite, chrysocolla, chalcocite and other secondary copper minerals.

FAMILY: MANGANESE CARBONATE

ID FACT FILE

CRYSTAL SYSTEM:
Hexagonal

COLOUR:
Raspberry or
rose-red to brown

WHERE:
Hydrothermal

ABUNDANCE:
Common

FORM:
Usually massive,
globular,
botryoidal; rare
crystals often
curved

CLEAVAGE:
Perfect

HARDNESS:
3.5–4.5

SG:
3.4–3.6

LUSTRE:
Vitreous to pearly

TRANSPARENCY:
Translucent

TESTS:
Uneven, brittle.
White streak

LOOKALIKES:
Dolomite

Rhodochrosite • $MnCO_3$

Chemical group: Carbonate

Rhodochrosite is a simple manganese
carbonate and a relative of siderite. It occurs in
hydrothermal vein systems and stockworks,
often associated with lead and silver-lead
minerals; it also occurs as a metasomatic
replacement in sedimentary rocks. Massive
forms often show wavy concentric successive
growth layers and distinctive pink colours.

FAMILY: MANGANESE CARBONATE

ID FACT FILE

CRYSTAL SYSTEM:
Hexagonal

COLOUR:
Yellowish, brown

WHERE:
Sedimentary,
hydrothermal

ABUNDANCE:
Common

FORM:
Tabular crystals
often slightly
curved; also
massive,
granular, or
oolitic

CLEAVAGE:
Perfect

HARDNESS:
4–4.5

SG:
3.7–3.9

LUSTRE:
Vitreous to pearly

TRANSPARENCY:
Translucent

TESTS:
Conchoidal,
brittle. White, or
brownish streak

LOOKALIKES:
Dolomite,
ankerite

Siderite • $FeCO_3$

Chemical group: Carbonate

Siderite, iron carbonate, occurs in
hydrothermal vein systems and stockworks, as
for rhodochrosite. It occurs most widely in
sedimentary rocks; it forms the ooliths in
oolitic ironstone, and beds and nodules in clay
ironstone especially of Carboniferous age. It
also occurs as a metasomatic replacement in
sedimentary rocks and can be an important
ore mineral of iron. An important rock-
forming mineral in some ironstone (*see*
p.224). Photograph shows cluster of tabular
crystals.

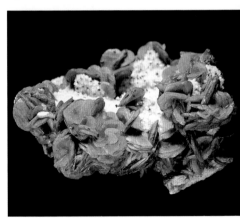

FAMILY: STRONTIUM CARBONATE

ID FACT FILE

CRYSTAL SYSTEM:
Orthorhombic

COLOUR:
Grey, white,
slightly tinted

WHERE:
Hydrothermal,
sedimentary,
igneous

ABUNDANCE:
Restricted

FORM:
Prismatic,
acicular, spiky or
fibrous crystals;
often twinned
like aragonite

CLEAVAGE:
Imperfect

HARDNESS:
3.5

SG:
3.7

LUSTRE:
Vitreous to
resinous

TRANSPARENCY:
Transparent to
opaque

TESTS:
Conchoidal,
brittle. White
streak

LOOKALIKES:
Aragonite is
lower density

Strontianite • SrCO$_3$

Chemical group: Carbonate

Strontianite occurs in hydrothermal vein
systems sometimes associated with fluorite,
galena and barite, as at type locality in
Strontian/Scotland, and Weardale/England. It
also occurs as nodules and as a replacement
mineral in sedimentary carbonate rocks
including Cretaceous marls and limestones in
Germany. Rarely as a primary mineral in
igneous carbonatites. It has higher SG than
many other carbonates.

FAMILY: BARIUM CARBONATE

Witherite • BaCO₃

Chemical group: Carbonate

ID FACT FILE

CRYSTAL SYSTEM:
Orthorhombic

COLOUR:
White with tints of grey, yellow or pink

WHERE:
Hydrothermal

ABUNDANCE:
Restricted

FORM:
Columnar crystals often twinned and pointed pseudohexagonal shapes; also massive

CLEAVAGE:
Poor

HARDNESS:
3–3.5

SG:
4.3

LUSTRE:
Vitreous to resinous

TRANSPARENCY:
Transparent to translucent

TESTS:
Uneven, brittle. White streak

LOOKALIKES:
Barite

Witherite occurs in hydrothermal vein systems sometimes as the matrix; often associated with galena and barite as at Alston Moor and Fallowfield in the north of England. Easily mistaken for barite when good crystal forms are absent. It has higher SG than most other carbonate minerals, including strontianite. Photograph shows pseudohexagonal crystals.

FAMILY: LEAD SULPHATE

ID FACT FILE

CRYSTAL SYSTEM:
Orthorhombic

COLOUR:
White with tints of grey, blue or yellow

WHERE:
Hydrothermal

ABUNDANCE:
Restricted

FORM:
Tabular, prismatic crystals; also granular or stalactitic

CLEAVAGE:
Imperfect

HARDNESS:
3–3.5

SG:
6.3–6.4

LUSTRE:
Adamantine, greasy

TRANSPARENCY:
Transparent to opaque

TESTS:
Conchoidal fracture, brittle. White streak

LOOKALIKES:
Barite

Anglesite • $PbSO_4$

Chemical group: Sulphate

Anglesite, lead sulphate, occurs commonly in the oxidation zone of hydrothermal systems containing galena in association with other carbonate minerals, as in Anglesey/Wales; also Cornwall and Cumberland/England, Austria and Spain. It usually forms small crystals and if sufficient in quantity has distinctive high density. Crystal faces often striated and often much smaller than barite, with which it may occur.

FAMILY: CALCIUM SULPHATE

ID FACT FILE

CRYSTAL SYSTEM:
Orthorhombic

COLOUR:
White with tints of grey, blue or yellow

WHERE:
Sedimentary

ABUNDANCE:
Rock-forming

FORM:
Tabular, prismatic crystals; also fibrous, massive or granular

CLEAVAGE:
Perfect giving rectangular fragments

HARDNESS:
3–3.5

SG:
2.9–3

LUSTRE:
Pearly

TRANSPARENCY:
Transparent to translucent

TESTS:
Conchoidal fracture, brittle. White streak

LOOKALIKES:
Halite is softer

Anhydrite • $CaSO_4$

Chemical group: Sulphate

Anhydrite changes slowly to gypsum through the addition of water. It occurs in salt deposits where, associated with gypsum, it often makes the impermeable cap rock. It may form alternating sedimentary layers with gypsum in evaporite deposits. Fibrous form (shown) easily distinguished from gypsum by greater hardness).

FAMILY: BARIUM SULPHATE

ID FACT FILE

CRYSTAL SYSTEM:
Orthorhombic

COLOUR:
Colourless, white with tints of yellow or pink; occasionally bluish

WHERE:
Hydrothermal, sedimentary

ABUNDANCE:
Common

FORM:
Tabular crystals often prominent terminations; also massive

CLEAVAGE:
Perfect parallel to length

HARDNESS:
3–3.5

SG:
4.5

LUSTRE:
Vitreous, pearly

TRANSPARENCY:
Transparent to translucent

TESTS:
Uneven, brittle. White streak

LOOKALIKES:
Witherite in massive form, celestine

Barite • BaSO$_4$

Chemical group: Sulphate

Barite, a common barium sulphate, is common as a secondary mineral in limestones, and as concretions and occasionally cement of sandstones as in Derbyshire/England and Elgin/Scotland respectively. It often contains calcium and strontium impurities and occurs commonly in hydrothermal vein deposits with lead and zinc minerals. It occurs in some igneous carbonatites. Where crystals are absent, the massive white form has distinctly high SG.

FAMILY: STRONTIUM SULPHATE

ID FACT FILE

CRYSTAL SYSTEM:
Orthorhombic

COLOUR:
White tinted pale
blue or yellow

WHERE:
Sedimentary,
hydrothermal

ABUNDANCE:
Rock-forming

FORM:
Tabular,
prismatic
crystals; also
fibrous, massive
or granular

CLEAVAGE:
Perfect

HARDNESS:
3–3.5

SG:
3.9–4.0

LUSTRE:
Vitreous, pearly

TRANSPARENCY:
Transparent to
translucent

TESTS:
Conchoidal
fracture, brittle.
White streak

LOOKALIKES:
Barite

Celestine • $SrSO_4$

Chemical group: Sulphate

Celestite, strontium sulphate, occurs as
sedimentary beds associated with gypsum and
halite in evaporite deposits. The beds are
typically nodular and uneven; celestite also
forms concretions in limestone. It occasionally
occurs in cavities in volcanic rocks, and is
associated with sulphur deposits in Sicily/Italy.
Also occurs as an accessory mineral in some
varieties of igneous carbonatite and pegmatite.

FAMILY; HYDRATED CALCIUM SULPHATE

ID FACT FILE

CRYSTAL SYSTEM:
Monoclinic

COLOUR:
Colourless,
white, grey,
yellowish or red

WHERE:
Sedimentary

ABUNDANCE:
Rock-forming

FORM:
Prismatic
twinned crystals
common; also
fibrous, massive
or granular

CLEAVAGE:
Perfect

HARDNESS:
1.5–2.0

SG:
2.3

LUSTRE:
Vitreous, pearly

TRANSPARENCY:
Transparent to
opaque

TESTS:
Conchoidal
fracture, brittle.
White streak

LOOKALIKES:
Crystals unlikely
to be mistaken

Gypsum • $CaSO_4.2H_2O$

Chemical group: Sulphate

Gypsum occurs throughout the world in salt
and evaporite deposits, and also as a
secondary mineral in some clays and
dolomitised limestones; impurities cause the
variation in colours. Alabaster is a snow-white
compact variety. Desert rose is an aggregate
of sand grains cemented by gypsum into a
rosette. Low hardness means it can be
scratched by a fingernail. Twinned crystals (as
illustrated) are common.

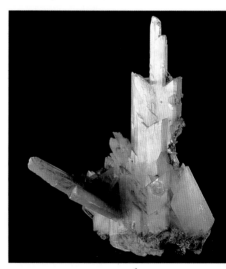

FAMILY: APATITE

ID FACT FILE

CRYSTAL SYSTEM:
Hexagonal

COLOUR:
Often pale green, bluish, or yellow; all colours

WHERE:
Igneous, metamorphic, sedimentary

ABUNDANCE:
Abundant

FORM:
Columnar or well-shaped elongated prisms; also massive, granular and radiating

CLEAVAGE:
Imperfect

HARDNESS:
5

SG:
3.16–3.22

LUSTRE:
Greasy, vitreous

TRANSPARENCY:
Transparent to opaque

TESTS:
Conchoidal, uneven, brittle fracture. White streak

LOOKALIKES:
Quartz

Apatite • $Ca_5(PO_4)_3F$

Chemical group: Phosphate

Apatite, or fluorapatite, occurs in small amounts in most igneous and metamorphic rocks. It also occurs in sedimentary rocks such as concretions in limestones. It can be a rock-forming mineral in marine bedded deposits. Chlorine can replace fluorine, and other impurities can include sodium and rare earth elements. Distinguished from quartz by lack of pointed crystal terminations and lower hardness.

FAMILY: LAZULITE

Lazulite •
$(Mg,Fe)Al_2(PO_4)_2(OH)_2$

Chemical group: Phosphate

ID FACT FILE

CRYSTAL SYSTEM:
Monoclinic

COLOUR:
Blue

WHERE:
Igneous

ABUNDANCE:
Uncommon

FORM:
Elongated
crystals

CLEAVAGE:
Poor

HARDNESS:
5.5–6

SG:
3.1–3.2

LUSTRE:
Vitreous,
adamantine

TRANSPARENCY:
Transparent to
opaque

TESTS:
Conchoidal,
uneven, brittle
fracture. White
streak

LOOKALIKES:
Azurite

Lazulite is an uncommon but distinctively blue-coloured magnesium-rich phosphate. It occurs in igneous rocks, in pegmatites. Some forms resemble spherulitic or radiating zeolites in appearance. Impurities can include calcium. Photograph shows an enlargement of a small crystal.

FAMILY: MONAZITE

ID FACT FILE

CRYSTAL SYSTEM:
Monoclinic

COLOUR:
White to dark
brown or green

WHERE:
Igneous,
metamorphic,
sedimentary

ABUNDANCE:
Common

FORM:
Thick tabular
crystals; also
massive

CLEAVAGE:
Perfect

HARDNESS:
5–5.5

SG:
4.6–5.7

LUSTRE:
Resinous

TRANSPARENCY:
Translucent to
opaque

TESTS:
Conchoidal,
brittle fracture.
White streak.
Radioactive

LOOKALIKES:
Apatite,
orthoclase

Monazite • $(Ce,La)PO_4$

Chemical group: Phosphate

Monazite is a rare earth element (Ce,La)
phosphate. It occurs as a minor constituent of
quartz-rich igneous rocks such as granites, in
some altered carbonatites and in pegmatites. It
also occurs in some metamorphic rocks like
gneiss; also in sedimentary placer deposits, as
in Brazil. It usually contains a small percentage
of thorium, making it mildly radioactive and a
valuable source for this element, in addition to
rare earth elements.

FAMILY: APATITE

Pyromorphite •
$Pb_5(PO_4)_3Cl$

Chemical group: Phosphate

ID FACT FILE

CRYSTAL SYSTEM:
Hexagonal

COLOUR:
Green, brown,
yellow; often
vivid colours

WHERE:
Igneous

ABUNDANCE:
Restricted

FORM:
Prismatic, barrel-
or needle-shaped
crystals; also
massive

CLEAVAGE:
None

HARDNESS:
3.5–4

SG:
6.7–7.1

LUSTRE:
Adamantine,
greasy

TRANSPARENCY:
Transparent to
translucent

TESTS:
Conchoidal,
uneven, brittle
fracture. White
streak

LOOKALIKES:
Apatite

Pyromorphite is a chlorophosphate which
occurs as a secondary mineral in the oxidation
zone of hydrothermal lead deposits, as in
Cornwall/England, Freiberg, Saxony and Harz/
Germany. Impurities include small amounts of
calcium or arsenic. Often associated with other
lead minerals including vanadinite, anglesite
and cerussite. High SG and rather bright
colours can be a guide to identification.

FAMILY: VIVIANITE

Vivianite •
$Fe_3(PO_4)_2.8H_2O$

Chemical group: Phosphate

ID FACT FILE

CRYSTAL SYSTEM:
Monoclinic

COLOUR:
Colourless,
white, blue or
green

WHERE:
Igneous,
sedimentary

ABUNDANCE:
Common

FORM:
Crystals tabular
or needle-like;
granular, or
earthy

CLEAVAGE:
Perfect

HARDNESS:
1.5–2

SG:
2.6–2.7

LUSTRE:
Vitreous, metallic

TRANSPARENCY:
Translucent

TESTS:
Fibrous brittle,
thin flexible.
White changing
to blue streak

LOOKALIKES:
Covellite, azurite

Vivianite is a hydrous iron phosphate. It
occurs in vein systems as a secondary
mineral associated with iron, tin and copper
deposits, as in Cornwall and Devon/England.
It also occurs in fossil bones and teeth, in
clay-rich rocks, in bogs, as in Scotland, and
in brown-coal deposits as in Germany. It is
easily distinguished from other lookalikes by
its translucent appearance and its notably low
hardness – it is easily scratched with a
fingernail.

FAMILY: AMPHIBOLE

Actinolite • $Ca_2Fe_5Si_8O_{22}(OH)_2$

Chemical group: Silicate

ID FACT FILE

CRYSTAL SYSTEM:
Monoclinic

COLOUR:
Green

WHERE:
Metamorphic

ABUNDANCE:
Common, rock-forming

FORM:
Slender bladed prisms or fibrous radiating bunches

CLEAVAGE:
Obvious parallel to length; two sets intersect at 120° on basal sections

HARDNESS:
5–6

SG:
2.9–3.2

LUSTRE:
Vitreous

TRANSPARENCY:
Opaque

TESTS:
White streak; splintery fracture

LOOKALIKES:
Hornblende

Actinolite is the iron-rich relative of tremolite amphibole and occurs as a common mineral in a wide variety of metamorphic rocks, including schists and greenschists; it often replaces pyroxene and hornblende in metamorphosed igneous rocks. The intersection of two cleavages at 120° on basal sections is distinctive of amphiboles. *Nephrite* is a tougher massive variety similar to jadeite.

FAMILY: AMPHIBOLE

Glaucophane • $Na_2(Mg, Fe)_3Al_2Si_8O_{22}(OH)_2$

Chemical group: Silicate

ID FACT FILE

CRYSTAL SYSTEM:
Monoclinic

COLOUR:
Blue or bluish grey

WHERE:
Metamorphic

ABUNDANCE:
Rare, rock-forming

FORM:
Bladed prisms, fibrous, massive or granular

CLEAVAGE:
Obvious parallel to length; two sets intersect at 120° on basal sections

HARDNESS:
6–6.5

SG:
3–3.1

LUSTRE:
Vitreous

TRANSPARENCY:
Translucent

TESTS:
Greyish streak

LOOKALIKES:
Riebeckite

Glaucophane is a sodium-rich amphibole, with more magnesium than iron. It has a distinctive blue colour and is a rock-forming mineral in rare high-pressure metamorphic areas where it forms blueschists, as in southern Brittany/France, Anglesey/Wales and Cyprus. Distinguished from blue riebeckite by the host rock type (riebeckite occurs in igneous rocks) and its greater hardness.

FAMILY: AMPHIBOLE

Hornblende • $(Ca,Mg,Fe,Na,Al)_7(Al,Si)_8O_{22}(OH)_2$

Chemical group: Silicate

ID FACT FILE

CRYSTAL SYSTEM:
Monoclinic

COLOUR:
Black with tints
of brown or green

WHERE:
Igneous,
metamorphic

ABUNDANCE:
Abundant

FORM:
Chunky prisms or
long bladed
crystals

CLEAVAGE:
Obvious parallel
to length; two
sets intersect at
120° on basal
sections

HARDNESS:
5–6

SG:
3–3.47

LUSTRE:
Vitreous

TRANSPARENCY:
Opaque to
translucent

TESTS:
Crystals often
twinned in
volcanic rocks.
Uneven fracture

LOOKALIKES:
Augite; where
twinned,
hornblende has
no re-entrant
angle

Hornblende is the commonest amphibole and occurs as a primary mineral in a wide variety of igneous rocks, often as well-formed crystals in volcanic rocks. It is also very common in regional metamorphic rocks derived from igneous rocks. The intersection of two cleavages at ~120° on basal sections is distinctive of amphiboles; also cross sections of prismatic crystals are often six-sided whereas augite is eight-sided.

FAMILY: AMPHIBOLE

Riebeckite •
$Na_2Fe_5Si_8O_{22}(OH)_2$

Chemical group: Silicate

ID FACT FILE

CRYSTAL SYSTEM:
Monoclinic

COLOUR:
Black, or dark blue

WHERE:
Igneous

ABUNDANCE:
Restricted

FORM:
Bladed prisms or fibrous radiating bunches

CLEAVAGE:
Obvious parallel to length; two sets intersect at 120° on basal sections

HARDNESS:
4

SG:
3.43

LUSTRE:
Vitreous

TRANSPARENCY:
Opaque

TESTS:
Uneven fracture, brittle, blue-grey streak

LOOKALIKES:
Hornblende is harder

Riebeckite is an alkali-amphibole rich in sodium and iron. Its occurrence is restricted to silica-rich igneous rocks such as riebeckite granite and riebeckite granophyre. It is the main dark rock-forming mineral in some small Scottish granites favoured for use in the ice-sport of curling. A finely fibrous pale greyish blue variety called crocidolite has separable fibres and resembles chrysotile; it is also known as blue asbestos, and is hazardous.

FAMILY: AMPHIBOLE

Tremolite •
$Ca_2Mg_5Si_8O_{22}(OH)_2$
Chemical group: Silicate

ID FACT FILE

CRYSTAL SYSTEM:
Monoclinic

COLOUR:
White

WHERE:
Metamorphic

ABUNDANCE:
Common

FORM:
Slender bladed prisms or fibrous radiating bunches

CLEAVAGE:
Obvious parallel to length; two sets intersect at 120° on basal sections

HARDNESS:
5–6

SG:
2.9–3.2

LUSTRE:
Vitreous

TRANSPARENCY:
Opaque

TESTS:
White colour distinguishes from other amphiboles

LOOKALIKES:
Hornblende and other amphiboles

Tremolite is the magnesium-rich relative of actinolite amphibole and occurs as a common mineral in a wide variety of metamorphic rocks. It is particularly characteristic of metamorphosed calcareous rocks, derived from impure limestones, including marbles and calc-silicate hornfelses. The typical ~120° cleavage intersection of amphiboles can be almost impossible to observe in small fibrous forms, even with a hand lens. Photograph shows fibrous or asbestiform variety.

FAMILY: FELDSPAR

ID FACT FILE

Crystal system:
Triclinic

Colour:
Colourless, white

Where:
Igneous,
metamorphic,
sedimentary

Abundance:
Rock-forming

Form:
Tabular crystals,
often twinned;
also massive,
granular

Cleavage:
Perfect

Hardness:
6–6.5

SG:
2.6–2.62

Lustre:
Vitreous to pearly

Transparency:
Transparent to
translucent

Tests:
Uneven fracture.
White streak

Lookalikes:
Orthoclase,
microcline

Albite • $NaAlSi_3O_8$

Chemical group: Alumino-silicate

The feldspar group is the most abundant mineral group in the Earth's crust, making up more than 60 per cent of the upper part. They are all alumino-silicates with varying amounts of the alkaline elements sodium, potassium and calcium. Albite is the pure sodium feldspar. It may contain some calcium. It occurs in a wide variety of igneous rocks including granite, syenite and pegmatites. It also occurs in metamorphic schists and gneisses, and is a common constituent of sedimentary arkose and impure sandstones. The variety cleavelandite occurs as platy white crystals in pegmatites.

FAMILY: PLAGIOCLASE FELDSPAR

ID FACT FILE

CRYSTAL SYSTEM:
Triclinic

COLOUR:
Colourless or white

WHERE:
Igneous, metamorphic

ABUNDANCE:
Rock-forming

FORM:
Prismatic crystals, often massive

CLEAVAGE:
Perfect

HARDNESS:
6–6.5

SG:
2.74

LUSTRE:
Vitreous to pearly

TRANSPARENCY:
Transparent to translucent

TESTS:
Conchoidal fracture. White streak

LOOKALIKES:
Albite, orthoclase

Anorthite • $CaAl_2Si_2O_8$

Chemical group: Alumino-silicate

Anorthite is the calcium-rich plagioclase usually with minor sodium and almost no potassium. It occurs in a few metamorphic hornfelses, but is typical of silica-poor igneous rocks like gabbro, troctolite, peridotite and norite; it is almost the sole constituent of the igneous rock anorthosite, as in Rhum /Scotland, and forming the bright, reflective highlands of the Moon. Photograph shows collection of igneous anorthite megacrysts.

FAMILY: FELDSPAR

ID FACT FILE

CRYSTAL SYSTEM:
Triclinic

COLOUR:
White, pink, yellow, grey

WHERE:
Igneous, sedimentary

ABUNDANCE:
Abundant

FORM:
Tabular crystals, often multiple twinning; also massive

CLEAVAGE:
Perfect

HARDNESS:
6

SG:
2.53–2.56

LUSTRE:
Vitreous to pearly

TRANSPARENCY:
Transparent to opaque

TESTS:
Conchoidal, uneven, brittle fracture. White streak

LOOKALIKES:
Albite, orthoclase

Microcline • $KAlSi_3O_8$

Chemical group: Alumino-silicate

Microcline is distinguished from orthoclase by fine parallel sets of striations on some faces (basal) due to multiple sets of twinning; otherwise physical properties are identical. Microcline occurs in coarse-grained very slowly-cooled igneous rocks like granites and pegmatites. A distinctive pale bluish green variety of microcline called *amazonite* is used as a semiprecious gem material.

FAMILY: FELDSPAR

ID FACT FILE

CRYSTAL SYSTEM:
Monoclinic

COLOUR:
White, pink,
yellow, grey

WHERE:
Igneous,
metamorphic,
sedimentary

ABUNDANCE:
Rock-forming

FORM:
Tabular crystals,
often twinned

CLEAVAGE:
Perfect; two sets
intersect at 90°
on some faces

HARDNESS:
6

SG:
2.53–2.56

LUSTRE:
Vitreous to pearly

TRANSPARENCY:
Transparent to
opaque

TESTS:
Conchoidal,
uneven, brittle
fracture. White
streak

LOOKALIKES:
Albite

Orthoclase • $KAlSi_3O_8$

Chemical group: Alumino-silicate

Orthoclase is the typical alkali feldspar with hardness of exactly 6. It is the dominant mineral in coarse-grained silica-rich igneous rocks like granite and syenite; it forms particularly large crystals in pegmatites. It sometimes contains impurities of barium. Common in many metamorphic rocks, it also occurs to a lesser extent in sedimentary rocks. The transparent variety *adularia* occurs in cavities in metamorphic rocks. Often distinguished from albite or plagioclase by pinkish colour.

Plagioclase • $CaAl_2Si_2O_8$ to $NaAlSi_3O_8$

Chemical group: Alumino-silicate

ID FACT FILE

CRYSTAL SYSTEM:
Triclinic

COLOUR:
Colourless, white, grey, greenish

WHERE:
Igneous, metamorphic, sedimentary

ABUNDANCE:
Rock-forming

FORM:
Prismatic, tabular crystals, multiply twinned

CLEAVAGE:
Perfect

HARDNESS:
6–6.5

SG:
2.61–2.77

LUSTRE:
Vitreous to pearly

TRANSPARENCY:
Transparent to translucent

TESTS:
Conchoidal, uneven, brittle fracture. White streak

LOOKALIKES:
Orthoclase

Plagioclase feldspars show complete compositional variation between sodium plagioclase, albite, and calcium plagioclase, anorthite (*see* separate entries, p.89 and p.90). Crystal shapes are generally tabular or prismatic and feature multiple twins parallel to length; sometimes visible with a hand lens on cleaved surfaces. Plagioclase occurs widely, primarily in igneous and metamorphic rocks worldwide. Compositions with 30–50 per cent albite (variety *labradorite*) often show an internal, oriented play of peacock colours (*schillerisation*) dominated by blues and greens.

FAMILY: FELDSPAR

Sanidine • KAlSi$_3$O$_8$

Chemical group: Alumino-silicate

ID FACT FILE

CRYSTAL SYSTEM:
Monoclinic

COLOUR:
Colourless,
white, grey

WHERE:
Igneous

ABUNDANCE:
Rock-forming

FORM:
Tabular crystals

CLEAVAGE:
Perfect

HARDNESS:
6

SG:
2.53–2.56

LUSTRE:
Vitreous to pearly

TRANSPARENCY:
Transparent to
opaque

TESTS:
Conchoidal,
uneven, brittle
fracture. White
streak. Simple
twins

LOOKALIKES:
Albite, orthoclase

Sanidine is the high-temperature form of orthoclase and is similarly sodium-poor. It occurs as prominent glassy crystals in some volcanic lavas like trachyte and phonolite. The sodium-rich equivalent is called *anorthoclase*, which belongs to the triclinic crystal system; it forms colourless to white crystals of slightly different shape, including prominent rhombs, as in the Permian volcanics near Oslo/Norway. Photograph shows twinned phenocrysts from volcanic rock.

FAMILY: FELDSPATHOID

Hauyne • $(Na,Ca)_{4-8}$ $Al_6Si_6(O,S)_{24}(SO_4,Cl)_{1-2}$

Chemical group: Aluminium silicate

ID FACT FILE

Crystal system:
Cubic

Colour:
Blue, dark blue, greenish blue; powdery blue

Where:
Igneous

Abundance:
Restricted

Form:
Small crystals with rounded or square outlines; aggregates

Cleavage:
Good

Hardness:
5.5–6

SG:
2.4–2.5

Lustre:
Vitreous, pearly

Transparency:
Translucent to opaque

Tests:
Conchoidal fracture. White streak

Lookalikes:
Sodalite

Hauyne usually forms aggregates of small crystals with a distinctive blue colour, generally less vivid than sodalite; on exposed rock surfaces it alters to a powdery whitish blue. Often occurs with similar composition mineral nosean. As for other feldspathoids (*see* nepheline, p.97) it occurs in igneous rocks that are low in silica and alkali-rich like phonolite, tephrite and melilitite. Hauyne is relatively common in young alkaline volcanic rocks such as Vesuvius, Naples/Italy and Eifel/Germany.

FAMILY: FELDSPATHOID

Leucite • KAlSi$_2$O$_6$

Chemical group: Potassium aluminium silicate

ID FACT FILE

CRYSTAL SYSTEM:
Tetragonal; cubic above 600°C/ 1112°F

COLOUR:
White, ash-grey

WHERE:
Igneous

ABUNDANCE:
Rock-forming

FORM:
Equant crystals with hexagonal or square outlines

CLEAVAGE:
None

HARDNESS:
5.5–6

SG:
2.45–2.5

LUSTRE:
Dull, vitreous, pearly

TRANSPARENCY:
Translucent to opaque

TESTS:
Conchoidal, brittle fracture. White streak

LOOKALIKES:
Garnet

Leucite is a potassium-rich feldspathoid (*see* nepheline, p.97). It is a major constituent of potassium-rich silica-poor volcanic rocks like phonolite, tephrite and leucite basalt. Its distinctive white crystals are particularly well known from many Italian volcanoes, including Vesuvius, Pompeii, Alban Hills and Roccamonfina; locally known as 'Vesuvian garnet'. Also found at Devon/England, southern Spain, France, Kaiserstuhl/Baden/ Germany.

FAMILY: FELDSPATHOID

Nepheline •
$(Na,K)AlSiO_4$

Chemical group: Alumino-silicate

ID FACT FILE

CRYSTAL SYSTEM:
Hexagonal

COLOUR:
White, yellowish, colourless

WHERE:
Igneous

ABUNDANCE:
Rock-forming

FORM:
Short prismatic crystals with prominent six-sided or square outlines; also massive in pegmatites

CLEAVAGE:
Poor

HARDNESS:
5.5–6

SG:
2.6–2.65

LUSTRE:
Vitreous, greasy

TRANSPARENCY:
Transparent to opaque

TESTS:
Conchoidal, uneven, brittle fracture. White streak

LOOKALIKES:
Quartz, melilite

Feldspathoids are alumino-silicates like feldspars, but have larger amounts of alkaline elements and less silica.

Nepheline is probably the most abundant feldspathoid. It always contains some potassium and a small excess of silica compared with the ideal composition. It is a major constituent of many alkaline igneous rocks like nepheline syenite and ijolite; it also occurs in alkaline volcanic rocks like nephelinite and phonolite, as in flood lavas in East Africa. It is prone to weathering and may develop crystal-shaped hollows on exposed rock surfaces.

FAMILY: FELDSPATHOID

Nosean •
$Na_8Al_6Si_6O_{24}(SO_4)$

Chemical group: Alumino-silicate

ID FACT FILE

CRYSTAL SYSTEM:
Cubic

COLOUR:
Grey, bluish,
yellowish

WHERE:
Igneous

ABUNDANCE:
Restricted

FORM:
Crystals with
squarish
outlines;
aggregates

CLEAVAGE:
Perfect

HARDNESS:
5.5

SG:
2.4–2.5

LUSTRE:
Vitreous, greasy

TRANSPARENCY:
Transparent to
opaque

TESTS:
Conchoidal
fracture. White
streak

LOOKALIKES:
Nepheline

Nosean is similar in appearance to nepheline,
with which it is often associated; it is also
similar in composition, except that it contains
sulphate. As for other feldspathoids (*see*
nepheline, p.97) nosean occurs in igneous rocks
that are low in silica and alkali-rich like syenite,
phonolite, tephrite and melilitite. Nosean is
locally common in young alkaline volcanic rocks
as at Naples/Italy and Laacher See /Eifel/
Germany.

FAMILY: FELDSPATHOID

Sodalite • $Na_4Al_3Si_3O_{12}Cl$

Chemical group: Sodium aluminium silicate

ID FACT FILE

CRYSTAL SYSTEM:
Cubic

COLOUR:
Lavender-blue, greyish blue, white, yellowish

WHERE:
Igneous

ABUNDANCE:
Rock-forming

FORM:
Equant crystals; aggregates or massive

CLEAVAGE:
Good

HARDNESS:
5–6

SG:
2.1–2.3

LUSTRE:
Vitreous, greasy

TRANSPARENCY:
Transparent to translucent

TESTS:
Uneven, conchoidal fracture. White streak

LOOKALIKES:
Hauyne

Sodalite is a chlorine-bearing feldspathoid that usually forms aggregates of small crystals, or massive areas with a distinctive clear blue colour, more vivid than hauyne. As for other feldspathoids (*see* nepheline, p.97) it occurs in igneous rocks that are low in silica and alkali-rich, such as syenite, phonolite, tephrite and melilitite. Sodalite can be a rock-forming mineral. Found also in alkaline volcanic rocks such as Vesuvius/Naples and Aeolian Islands/Italy, and Eifel/Germany. A sky-blue variety of sodalite, called *lazurite*, is the chief constituent of the blue gem material *lapis lazuli*, found in Chile and Afghanistan.

FAMILY: GARNET

Almandine •
$Fe_3Al_2(SiO_4)_3$
Chemical group: Silicate

Almandine is the commonest type of garnet occurring in metamorphic rocks such as mica-schists and garnet gneisses. Also referred to as 'common garnet' which is brownish red, the translucent attractive deep-red variety is semi-precious, and therefore sought after in recent detrital deposits where it is often rounded. The lack of cleavage, combined with high hardness and resistance to weathering, means garnet is often present as a 'heavy mineral' in sediments. A brown relative particularly rich in manganese called 'spessartine' is uncommon.

ID FACT FILE

CRYSTAL SYSTEM:
Cubic

COLOUR:
Deep red

WHERE:
Metamorphic

ABUNDANCE:
Very common

FORM:
Euhedral equant cubic crystals often with good crystal faces (rhombododeca-hedron = 12 faces, trapezohedron = 24 faces)

CLEAVAGE:
None

HARDNESS:
6.5–7.5

SG:
3.9–4.2

LUSTRE:
Vitreous

TRANSPARENCY:
Opaque to translucent or deep red transparent

TESTS:
Subconchoidal or uneven fracture. Relatively high density for silicate minerals

LOOKALIKES:
Garnets

FAMILY: GARNET

Andradite •
$Ca_3Fe_2(SiO_4)_3$

Chemical group: Silicate

ID FACT FILE

CRYSTAL SYSTEM:
Cubic

COLOUR:
Dark brown, greenish or yellowish brown

WHERE: .
Metamorphic

ABUNDANCE:
Common

FORM:
Euhedral equant cubic crystals often with good crystal faces called rhombododeca-hedron (12 faces) or trapezohedron (24 faces)

CLEAVAGE:
None

HARDNESS:
7.0 or greater

SG:
3.8

LUSTRE:
Vitreous

TRANSPARENCY:
Opaque

TESTS:
Subconchoidal or uneven fracture. Relatively high density for silicate minerals

LOOKALIKES:
Garnets

Andradite is the calcium-rich and generally less attractive relative of common garnet (almandine) except for a bright green gem variety called *demantoid* (illustrated). It occurs generally in metamorphic rocks, though a black variety called melanite occurs in alkaline igneous rocks such as nepheline syenites. As for all garnets, distinctive features in well crystalline forms may include characteristic garnet shape (*see* Form) and absence of cleavage and twinning. Photograph shows natural and cut gem forms.

FAMILY: GARNET

ID FACT FILE

CRYSTAL SYSTEM:
Cubic

COLOUR:
Pale green,
greenish white

WHERE:
Metamorphic

ABUNDANCE:
Restricted

FORM:
Euhedral equant
cubic crystals
often with good
crystal faces
(rhombododeca-
hedron = 12
faces)

CLEAVAGE:
None

HARDNESS:
Just harder than
quartz (i.e. 7)

SG:
3.5

LUSTRE:
Vitreous

TRANSPARENCY:
Opaque to
translucent

TESTS:
Conchoidal or
uneven fracture
(soluble in
hydrochloric acid)

LOOKALIKES:
Garnets

Grossular • $Ca_3Al_2(SiO_4)_3$

Chemical group: Silicate

Grossular is a calcium-rich garnet
characteristic of metamorphosed impure
limestones or marble. Semiprecious
transparent varieties with yellowish or
pinkish colour occasionally occur. It can
occur at the contact between igneous rocks
and older rocks in *skarn*. Photograph shows
natural and cut gem forms.

FAMILY: GARNET

ID FACT FILE

CRYSTAL SYSTEM:
Cubic

COLOUR:
Deep crimson-red with violet tints

WHERE:
Metamorphic

ABUNDANCE:
Restricted

FORM:
Euhedral equant cubic crystals often rounded

CLEAVAGE:
None

HARDNESS:
7.5

SG:
3.7

LUSTRE:
Vitreous

TRANSPARENCY:
Translucent to transparent

TESTS:
Conchoidal

LOOKALIKES:
Garnets

Pyrope • $Mg_3Al_2(SiO_4)_3$

Chemical group: Silicate

Pyrope is the magnesium-rich red garnet found in metamorphosed ultrabasic igneous rocks and is stable to very high pressures. It is characteristic of olivine-rich rocks like peridotite and lherzolite. It is present in the deepest samples of the Earth's upper mantle. Photograph shows group of partly rounded large crystals and a cut gem.

FAMILY: MICA

Biotite • $K(Mg,Fe)_3$ $(Al,Fe)Si_3O_{10}(OH,F)_2$

Chemical group: Hydrous silicate

ID FACT FILE

CRYSTAL SYSTEM:
Monoclinic

COLOUR:
Black, dark brown

WHERE:
Metamorphic, igneous

ABUNDANCE:
Rock-forming

FORM:
Hexagonal-shaped crystals; aggregates

CLEAVAGE:
Perfect

HARDNESS:
2.5–3

SG:
2.7–3.3

LUSTRE:
Vitreous, pearly, metallic

TRANSPARENCY:
Transparent to opaque

TESTS:
Platy fracture, flexible. White streak

LOOKALIKES:
Phlogopite, chlorite

Biotite is an important constituent of many igneous rocks, like granite, diorite and andesite. It is also a rock-forming mineral in metamorphic rocks like gneiss, schist and hornfels. It contains variable amounts of magnesium and iron and may contain small amounts of titanium. It often weathers to a pale golden colour, when it resembles phlogopite (*see* p.107).

FAMILY: MICA

Lepidolite • $K(Li,Al)_3 (Si,Al)_4 O_{10} (F,OH)_2$

Chemical group: Hydrous silicate

ID FACT FILE

CRYSTAL SYSTEM:
Monoclinic

COLOUR:
Violet, rose-pink

WHERE:
Igneous

ABUNDANCE:
Restricted

FORM:
Hexagonal-shaped crystals; platy aggregates

CLEAVAGE:
Perfect

HARDNESS:
2–3

SG:
2.8–2.9

LUSTRE:
Pearly, vitreous

TRANSPARENCY:
Transparent to translucent

TESTS:
Platy fracture, elastic, flexible. White streak

LOOKALIKES:
Unlikely to be mistaken

Lepidolite is a lithium-rich mica, usually with very distinctive violet to pink colour. It occurs in silica-rich igneous rocks like granite and pegmatite, and is often associated with other lithium-bearing minerals like tourmaline, as in Cornwall/England, California/USA, and Minas Gerias/Brazil. Like all micas, it has perfect cleavage, and individual flakes can be separated with a fingernail.

FAMILY: MICA

Muscovite •
$KAl_2(Si_3Al)O_{10}(OH)_2$

Chemical group: Hydrous silicate

ID FACT FILE

CRYSTAL SYSTEM:
Monoclinic

COLOUR:
Colourless,
lightly tinted

WHERE:
Metamorphic,
igneous,
sedimentary

ABUNDANCE:
Rock-forming

FORM:
Hexagonal-
shaped crystals;
platy aggregates

CLEAVAGE:
Perfect

HARDNESS:
2–3

SG:
2.8–2.9

LUSTRE:
Pearly, metallic

TRANSPARENCY:
Transparent to
translucent

TESTS:
Platy fracture,
flexible. White
streak

LOOKALIKES:
Phlogopite

Like all micas, muscovite reflects light strongly
from broken platy fragments (cleavage flakes)
and glistens. It occurs as an essential
constituent of silica-rich igneous rocks like
granite, greisen and pegmatite. It occurs
widely in metamorphic rocks like gneiss and
mica-schist. It is a common mineral resistant to
weathering and occurs in sedimentary rocks
like micaceous sandstone. *Sericite* is a clay-like
variety formed by alteration of feldspars.
Muscovite concentrations are found in Russia,
India, USA and Canada.

FAMILY: MICA

Phlogopite •
$KMg_3AlSi_3O_{10}(F,OH)_2$

Chemical group: Hydrous silicate

ID FACT FILE

CRYSTAL SYSTEM:
Monoclinic

COLOUR:
Pale brown,
reddish brown,
grey

WHERE:
Metamorphic,
igneous

ABUNDANCE:
Rock-forming

FORM:
Hexagonal-
shaped crystals;
aggregates

CLEAVAGE:
Perfect

HARDNESS:
2.5–3

SG:
2.7–2.9

LUSTRE:
Pearly, metallic

TRANSPARENCY:
Transparent to
translucent

TESTS:
Platy fracture,
flexible. White
streak

LOOKALIKES:
Biotite,
muscovite

Phlogopite is a magnesium-rich mica. It is a paler colour than biotite and sometimes has a golden tint. It is a primary constituent of ultrabasic igneous rocks like kimberlite, carbonatite and lamprophyre. It also occurs in metamorphic rocks like impure marble. It usually contains impurities of iron and some titanium. Found in Canada, Baikal/Russia, Sweden, Finland and Scotland.

FAMILY: OLIVINE

Olivine • $(Mg,Fe)_2SiO_4$

Chemical group: Silicate

ID FACT FILE

CRYSTAL SYSTEM:
Orthorhombic

COLOUR:
Green, olive-green, rarely other colours

WHERE:
Igneous, metamorphic

ABUNDANCE:
Rock-forming

FORM:
Stubby prismatic crystals, also granular aggregates

CLEAVAGE:
Poor

HARDNESS:
6.5–7

SG:
3.27–4.20

LUSTRE:
Vitreous to greasy

TRANSPARENCY:
Transparent to translucent

TESTS:
Conchoidal, brittle fracture. White streak

LOOKALIKES:
Chrome diopside (p.111)

Olivine shows a complete compositional variation between forsterite (iron-free) and fayalite (magnesium-free). Typical green olivine with mixed iron and magnesium is the main mineral forming peridotites. It occurs in igneous rocks with low silica such as gabbro, basalt, dolerite; it forms slender crystals in komatiite. *Forsterite* can occur in metamorphic marble. *Fayalite* is dark brown or black; it is uncommon but can occur in granite pegmatites. The pale green semiprecious gem variety *peridote* is transparent, as found in Egypt, New Mexico and Brazil.

FAMILY: PYROXENE

Aegirine • NaFe Si$_2$O$_6$

Chemical group: Silicate

ID FACT FILE

CRYSTAL SYSTEM:
Monoclinic

COLOUR:
Dark green to brown

WHERE:
Igneous

ABUNDANCE:
Common

FORM:
Prismatic crystals, acicular or radiating bunches

CLEAVAGE:
Distinctive parallel along prisms

HARDNESS:
6–6.5

SG:
3.5

LUSTRE:
Vitreous

TRANSPARENCY:
Opaque to translucent

TESTS:
Strongly coloured and easily distinguished in thin sections

LOOKALIKES:
Augite

Aegirine is a sodium ferric iron pyroxene that forms a compositional gradation into augite. It can form radiating clusters or 'rosettes'. Basal sections show 90° cleavage intersection of pyroxene. The intermediate pyroxene, *aegirine-augite*, is black, and occurs widely in alkaline volcanic and igneous rocks, such as phonolites. Aegirine is characteristic of late-stage alkaline pegmatites and strongly alkaline plutonic igneous rocks such as nepheline syenites.

FAMILY: PYROXENE

ID FACT FILE

CRYSTAL SYSTEM:
Monoclinic

COLOUR:
Black or greenish black

WHERE:
Igneous and metamorphic

ABUNDANCE:
Abundant

FORM:
Short prismatic or elongate bladed crystals; sometimes irregular-shaped

CLEAVAGE:
Distinctive parallel along the length of crystals

HARDNESS:
5–6

SG:
3.2–3.5

LUSTRE:
Vitreous to resinous

TRANSPARENCY:
Opaque

TESTS:
Diagnostic pyroxene cleavage. May show simple twinning

LOOKALIKES:
Hornblende

Augite • $(Ca,Mg,Fe,Al)_2$ $(Si,Al)_2O_6$

Chemical group: Silicate

Augite is the commonest pyroxene, occurring widely in igneous rocks. It forms stumpy prismatic crystals in volcanic rocks, and longer flat-bladed crystals in basic dykes and sills such as dolerites. It also occurs in high-grade metamorphic rocks such as pyroxene-granulites. Basal sections show 90° cleavage intersection of pyroxene. Single crystals distinguished from hornblende by re-entrant angle when twinned, as along top edge of right-hand crystal shown.

FAMILY: PYROXENE

Diopside • CaMg Si$_2$O$_6$

Chemical group: Silicate

ID FACT FILE

CRYSTAL SYSTEM:
Monoclinic

COLOUR:
White, green or
dark green

WHERE:
Igneous and
metamorphic

ABUNDANCE:
Common

FORM:
Prismatic
crystals or
equant grains

CLEAVAGE:
Distinctive
parallel to length
of prisms

HARDNESS:
5–6

SG:
3.2–3.4

LUSTRE:
Vitreous to
resinous

TRANSPARENCY:
Opaque to
transparent

TESTS:
Diagnostic
pyroxene
cleavage. Green
colour of chrome-
rich variety
distinctive

LOOKALIKES:
Distinguished
from sometimes
coexisting olivine
by cleavage

Diopside is the magnesium-rich relative of
hedenbergite. It is a monoclinic pyroxene or
clinopyroxene. It typically occurs in
metamorphosed impure limestones and marbles,
where its pale green colour may be distinctive. It
also occurs in ultrabasic, metamorphic rocks
such as lherzolites and wherlites, where the
chromium-rich variety, *chrome-diopside*, has a
vibrant apple-green colour. Below: several
crystals with basal 90° pyroxene cleavage.

FAMILY: PYROXENE

Enstatite • $Mg_2Si_2O_6$

Chemical group: Silicate

ID FACT FILE

CRYSTAL SYSTEM:
Orthorhombic

COLOUR:
Brown, bronze, grey

WHERE:
Igneous and metamorphic

ABUNDANCE:
Abundant

FORM:
Short prismatic or elongate bladed crystals; sometimes irregular-shaped

CLEAVAGE:
Distinctive parallel along the length of crystals. Basal prismatic sections show 90° cleavage intersection of pyroxene

HARDNESS:
5.5

SG:
3.1–3.3

LUSTRE:
Vitreous to pearly

TRANSPARENCY:
Translucent to opaque

TESTS:
Diagnostic pyroxene cleavage

LOOKALIKES:
Augite

Enstatite is an orthorhombic pyroxene or orthopyroxene. It occurs widely in ultrabasic, basic and intermediate igneous rocks such as pyroxenites, gabbros and norites. The iron-bearing variety, *bronzite*, has a pearly metallic lustre resembling bronze, and is often characteristic of serpentinised ultrabasic rocks such as wherlites and peridotites. Enstatite is also an important mineral in many meteorites.

FAMILY: PYROXENE

Hedenbergite •
CaFeSi₂O₆

Chemical group: Silicate

ID FACT FILE

CRYSTAL SYSTEM:
Monoclinic

COLOUR:
Black

WHERE:
Metamorphic or igneous

ABUNDANCE:
Uncommon

FORM:
Prismatic or bladed crystals

CLEAVAGE:
Obvious parallel along the length of crystals; basal sections show 90° cleavage intersection of pyroxene

HARDNESS:
6

SG:
3.7

LUSTRE:
Vitreous

TRANSPARENCY:
Opaque

TESTS:
Restricted occurrence

LOOKALIKES:
Augite

Hedenbergite is a relatively uncommon calcium iron silicate occurring as a contact metamorphic mineral in skarns developed specifically between high-temperature igneous rocks and calcareous country rocks. It is usually associated with iron-rich silicates and other iron minerals in skarns. It also occurs in basic igneous rocks on the Moon.

FAMILY: PYROXENE

Hypersthene •
$(Mg,Fe)_2Si_2O_6$

Chemical group: Silicate

ID FACT FILE

CRYSTAL SYSTEM:
Orthorhombic

COLOUR:
Brown, black or
greenish black

WHERE:
Igneous and
metamorphic

ABUNDANCE:
Abundant

FORM:
Often massive,
sometimes
prismatic

CLEAVAGE:
Distinctive
parallel along the
length of crystals

HARDNESS:
5–6

SG:
3.4–3.5

LUSTRE:
Sub-metallic

TRANSPARENCY:
Translucent to
opaque

TESTS:
Diagnostic
pyroxene
cleavage.
Uneven fracture,
brittle

LOOKALIKES:
Bronzite
distinguished by
colour and lustre

Hypersthene is a mixed iron-magnesium silicate that occurs in basic and intermediate igneous rocks such as norite and hypersthene-andesite. It also occurs widely in metamorphic rocks including high-grade regional charnockites and contact metamorphic hornfelses. Its subtle pink-green colours in thin section are distinctive. Basal prismatic sections show 90° cleavage intersection of pyroxene.

FAMILY: PYROXENE

Jadeite • $NaAlSi_2O_6$

Chemical group: Silicate

ID FACT FILE

CRYSTAL SYSTEM:
Monoclinic

COLOUR:
Green, white

WHERE:
Metamorphic

ABUNDANCE:
Common

FORM:
Massive, fibrous

CLEAVAGE:
Imperfect

HARDNESS:
6.5–7

SG:
3.3–3.36

LUSTRE:
Vitreous

TRANSPARENCY:
Translucent to opaque

TESTS:
Uneven, brittle fracture; very tough. White streak

LOOKALIKES:
Amphibole, aegirine

Jadeite is a variety of pyroxene and may have a composition part way towards aegirine. Its toughness and range of green colours are well known from its use as an ornamental and gem stone. It occurs in metamorphic schist, as in China, Japan and California/USA. Jade is a common term used for semiprecious jadeite and another mineral with similar properties called nephrite (variety of actinolite). Photograph shows natural jadeite and a polished gem.

FAMILY: PYROXENOID

Pectolite • $Ca_2NaH(SiO_3)_3$

Chemical group: Silicate

ID FACT FILE

CRYSTAL SYSTEM:
Monoclinic

COLOUR:
White

WHERE:
Metamorphic,
hydrothermal,
igneous

ABUNDANCE:
Common

FORM:
Radiating,
fibrous or
massive

CLEAVAGE:
Not prominent

HARDNESS:
5

SG:
2.7–2.9

LUSTRE:
Silky when
fibrous

TRANSPARENCY:
Opaque

TESTS:
White streak

LOOKALIKES:
Zeolite family

Pectolite is a fairly common white mineral occurring during hydrothermal alteration of igneous and volcanic rocks, such as in amygdales (filled gas cavities or vesicles). It is usually associated with other zeolite minerals. It can also occur in igneous pegmatite. Radiating groups of elongated crystals are typical but easily mistaken for zeolites, especially where small crystal size requires use of a hand-lens.

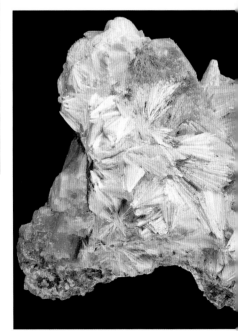

FAMILY: PYROXENOID

ID FACT FILE

CRYSTAL SYSTEM:
Triclinic

COLOUR:
Pink, red;
oxidises black

WHERE:
Metamorphic,
igneous

ABUNDANCE:
Restricted

FORM:
Massive, fibrous;
tabular crystals

CLEAVAGE:
Perfect

HARDNESS:
5.5–6.5

SG:
3.4–3.73

LUSTRE:
Vitreous, pearly

TRANSPARENCY:
Translucent to
opaque

TESTS:
Uneven, brittle
fracture; tough
when massive.
White streak

LOOKALIKES:
Rose quartz,
rhodochrosite

Rhodonite • $Mn_2Si_2O_6$

Chemical group: Silicate

Crystals of rhodonite are rare. Its bright pink
to reddish colour may be obscured by black
colours developed by oxidation. Impurities
commonly include some calcium and iron. It
occurs in hydrothermal vein systems
associated with lead-silver veins and other
manganese minerals, like rhodochrosite; also
in some metamorphic rocks like schist. It
occurs in France, India, USA and
Urals/Russia. Less hard than quartz.

FAMILY: PYROXENE

ID FACT FILE

CRYSTAL SYSTEM:
Monoclinic

COLOUR:
Grey, white, pale green, pink

WHERE:
Igneous

ABUNDANCE:
Restricted

FORM:
Prismatic, tabular crystals; also massive

CLEAVAGE:
Perfect

HARDNESS:
6–7

SG:
3.16–3.2

LUSTRE:
Vitreous, pearly

TRANSPARENCY:
Transparent to translucent

TESTS:
Uneven fracture. White streak

LOOKALIKES:
Orthoclase

Spodumene • LiAlSi$_2$O$_6$

Chemical group: Silicate

Spodumene occurs in granite pegmatite, often accompanied by other lithium minerals like lepidolite and tourmaline. It may form large crystals with shiny cleavage surfaces. Transparent coloured varieties used for gemstones are yellowish green *hiddenite* and pink to violet *kunzite*. Photograph shows natural tabular crystal and cut gem.

FAMILY: PYROXENOID

Wollastonite • CaSiO₃

Chemical group: Silicate

Wollastonite is a simple calcium silicate of the pyroxenoid family. It is always white or pale-coloured, often massive but can occur as tabular crystals. It occurs commonly in contact metamorphosed impure limestones and marbles. It also occurs in alkaline silicate volcanic rocks associated with carbonatites.

ID FACT FILE

CRYSTAL SYSTEM:
Triclinic

COLOUR:
White, grey or brownish

WHERE:
Metamorphic and igneous

ABUNDANCE:
Common

FORM:
Tabular crystals, sometimes massive or fibrous

CLEAVAGE:
Obvious good cleavage

HARDNESS:
4.5–5

SG:
2.8–2.9

LUSTRE:
Vitreous

TRANSPARENCY:
Translucent

TESTS:
Breaks rather easily along the cleavage

LOOKALIKES:
None

FAMILY: SERPENTINE

ID FACT FILE

CRYSTAL SYSTEM:
Monoclinic

COLOUR:
Green, yellowish green

WHERE:
Metamorphic

ABUNDANCE:
Rock-forming

FORM:
Crystals unknown; massive, scaly, platy

CLEAVAGE:
Perfect

HARDNESS:
2.5–4

SG:
2.0–2.6

LUSTRE:
Greasy, dull

TRANSPARENCY:
Translucent to opaque

TESTS:
Conchoidal, flaky fracture. White streak. Massive serpentine. Can be cut with a knife

LOOKALIKES:
Other serpentine minerals

Antigorite • $(Mg,Fe)_3Si_2O_5(OH)_4$

Chemical group: Hydrous magnesium silicate

Antigorite is an iron-bearing form of serpentine, the iron usually lending a darker colour to this mineral compared with iron-free varieties like chrysotile. A massive variety with dark reddish brown to green colours is called *lizardite*. It occurs in magnesium-rich metamorphic rocks called serpentinite, usually derived from ultrabasic igneous rocks rich in olivine and pyroxene. Found in Cornwall/England, Harz/Germany, Cyprus, E. Canada, South Africa and Zimbabwe.

FAMILY: SERPENTINE

Chrysotile •
$Mg_3Si_2O_5(OH)_4$

Chemical group: Hydrous magnesium silicate

ID FACT FILE

CRYSTAL SYSTEM:
Monoclinic

COLOUR:
Green, grey, white

WHERE:
Metamorphic

ABUNDANCE:
Rock-forming

FORM:
Crystals unknown; fibrous aggregates, asbestos

CLEAVAGE:
Perfect, separable fibres

HARDNESS:
2.5–4

SG:
2.0–2.6

LUSTRE:
Greasy, dull

TRANSPARENCY:
Translucent to opaque

TESTS:
Splintery fracture. White streak

LOOKALIKES:
Distinctive fibrous mineral

Chrysotile is the fibrous form of serpentine, with fine or coarse fibres occurring in veins and lenses in massive varieties of metamorphic serpentine (serpentinite rock). Aggregates with parallel fibres are called *asbestos*. The mineral also occurs in veins in some impure marbles. Impurities can include small amounts of iron and manganese. Found in Cornwall/England, Harz/Germany, Cyprus, E. Canada, South Africa and Zimbabwe. Photograph shows asbestos chrysotile.

FAMILY: QUARTZ

ID FACT FILE

CRYSTAL SYSTEM:
Trigonal

COLOUR:
White, bluish, coloured

WHERE:
Sedimentary, igneous

ABUNDANCE:
Abundant

FORM:
Microcrystalline varieties of quartz; fibrous, massive

CLEAVAGE:
None

HARDNESS:
6.5–7

SG:
2.58–2.65

LUSTRE:
Waxy, dull

TRANSPARENCY:
Translucent

TESTS:
Conchoidal fracture. White streak. Crystals not visible to naked eye. Porous and permeable by dyes

LOOKALIKES:
Zeolites

Quartz-chalcedony • SiO_2

Chemical group: Silica

The many forms of chalcedony are all varieties of microcrystalline quartz, often partly hydrated. Crystals are not visible. They occur as nodules in sedimentary rocks, and as infilling of cavities in igneous rocks and mineralised vein systems. *Carnelian* is translucent yellowish red; *jasper* is brown-red or rarely green; *blood stone* is bright green speckled with red; *agate* is composed of different coloured bands; *flint* is black to grey, and *chert* is similar but lacking conchoidal fracture.

FAMILY: QUARTZ

ID FACT FILE

CRYSTAL SYSTEM:
Trigonal

COLOUR:
White, various colours; opalescent

WHERE:
Sedimentary, igneous

ABUNDANCE:
Uncommon

FORM:
Microcrystalline varieties of quartz; fibrous, massive

CLEAVAGE:
None

HARDNESS:
5.5–6

SG:
1.98–2.5

LUSTRE:
Vitreous, greasy

TRANSPARENCY:
Transparent to opaque

TESTS:
Conchoidal fracture. White streak. Crystals not visible to naked eye

LOOKALIKES:
Quartz-chalcedony

Opal • $SiO_2.nH_2O$

Chemical group: Hydrous silica

Opal lacks almost any crystalline structure (amorphous). It contains up to 30 per cent water, and is lighter and softer than quartz. It occurs filling fractures in igneous rocks and as crusts and nodules in sedimentary rocks. There are many variety names and colours and most show an internal play of colours with rainbow tints called opalescence (as illustrated); common opal, *hyalite*, is glassy and almost colourless; *precious opal*, like *fire-opal*, shows spectacular opalescence. Gem-quality opal is obtained from Mexico and especially from Australia.

FAMILY: QUARTZ

ID FACT FILE

CRYSTAL SYSTEM:
Trigonal

COLOUR:
Colourless, white

WHERE:
Igneous,
metamorphic,
sedimentary

ABUNDANCE:
Rock-forming

FORM:
Pointed, six-
sided prismatic
crystals; also
massive

CLEAVAGE:
None

HARDNESS:
7

SG:
2.65

LUSTRE:
Vitreous, greasy

TRANSPARENCY:
Transparent to
opaque

TESTS:
Conchoidal
fracture. White
streak

LOOKALIKES:
Feldspars

Quartz • SiO_2

Chemical group: Silica

Quartz is the second most abundant rock-forming mineral after feldspar. It occurs widely in silica-rich igneous rocks like granite. There are several different polymorphs of quartz; in high-temperature igneous rocks it forms *tridymite* (*see* opposite) and *cristobalite*; in very high-pressure impact metamorphic rocks it forms *coesite* and *stishovite*. It is resistant to weathering and accumulates in sands as well as in sedimentary rocks like sandstone. It is widely distributed in metamorphic rocks like gneiss, migmatite and quartzite. Quartz also occurs as a prominent matrix mineral in hydrothermal vein systems. There are many named varieties of quartz, due to its different colours and forms; *rock crystal* is colourless, *amethyst* is purple and *citrine* is yellow (*see* opposite).

FAMILY: QUARTZ

Top: Tridymite
Middle left: Citrine, cut gem
Middle right: Amethyst
Bottom: Twins

FAMILY: ZEOLITE

Analcime •
$NaAlSi_2O_6.H_2O$

Chemical group: Hydrous silicate

ID FACT FILE

CRYSTAL SYSTEM:
Orthorhombic
(nearly cubic)

COLOUR:
Milky white, tints
of pale green,
yellow or pink

WHERE:
Igneous

ABUNDANCE:
Abundant

FORM:
Equant crystals;
granular
aggregates

CLEAVAGE:
None

HARDNESS:
5–5.5

SG:
2.24–2.31

LUSTRE:
Vitreous

TRANSPARENCY:
Transparent to
opaque

TESTS:
Conchoidal,
uneven fracture.
White streak

LOOKALIKES:
Nepheline

Analcime occurs as a primary mineral in some
alkaline igneous rocks like dolerite, alkali basalt
and phonolite. It also occurs in typical zeolitic
form as a secondary hydrous alteration of
feldspars and feldspathoids, filling cavities,
cracks and spaces in volcanic lavas and other
igneous rocks. Found in Scotland, Ireland,
Germany, France, Italy.

FAMILY: APOPHYLLITE

ID FACT FILE

CRYSTAL SYSTEM:
Tetragonal

COLOUR:
Pale green, white
or pale colours

WHERE:
Igneous,
metamorphic

ABUNDANCE:
Common

FORM:
Pointed crystals
with square
cross sections

CLEAVAGE:
Perfect

HARDNESS:
4.5–5

SG:
2.3–2.4

LUSTRE:
Pearly, vitreous

TRANSPARENCY:
Translucent to
transparent

TESTS:
Uneven, brittle
fracture. White
streak

LOOKALIKES:
Datolite, zeolites

Apophyllite* •
$KCa_4Si_8O_{20}F.8H_2O$

Chemical group: Hydrous silicate

Apophyllite is a fairly common mineral
growing as clusters of crystals protruding into
voids in lava flows. It also occurs in some
hydrothermal mineral veins. It often occurs
together with other zeolite minerals in
hydrothermally altered basalts as in Scotland,
Germany and India.

   *Apophyllite often contains chlorine in place
of some fluorine; depending on which is
dominant it is more accurately called
fluorapophyllite or chlorapophyllite.

FAMILY: ZEOLITE

Harmotome • $(Ba,K)\sim_2$ $(Si,Al)_8O_{16}.6H_2O$

Chemical group: Hydrous silicate

ID FACT FILE

CRYSTAL SYSTEM:
Monoclinic

COLOUR:
White, grey

WHERE:
Igneous

ABUNDANCE:
Common

FORM:
Prismatic
crystals, cross-
like twinning

CLEAVAGE:
Imperfect

HARDNESS:
4.5

SG:
2.44–2.50

LUSTRE:
Vitreous

TRANSPARENCY:
Translucent,
cloudy

TESTS:
Uneven, brittle
fracture. White
streak

LOOKALIKES:
Analcime,
zeolites

Harmotome is a potassium-rich zeolite, usually with some barium. It occurs in hydrothermal mineral veins associated with other barium- or strontium-rich minerals, as at Strontian/ Scotland. As with other zeolites it also occurs as secondary infillings in voids, cracks and veins in altered volcanic rocks. Found in Idar-Oberstein and Harz/Germany, Kongsberg/Norway, France and Italy.

FAMILY: ZEOLITE

Heulandite • $(Ca,Na)_{2-3}$ $Al_3(Al,Si)_2Si_{13}O_{36} \cdot 12H_2O$

Chemical group: Hydrous silicate

ID FACT FILE

CRYSTAL SYSTEM:
Monoclinic

COLOUR:
White, red,
brown

WHERE:
Igneous,
metamorphic

ABUNDANCE:
Common

FORM:
Tabular crystals,
lamellar
aggregates,
radiating;
globular

CLEAVAGE:
Perfect

HARDNESS:
3.5–4

SG:
2.2

LUSTRE:
Vitreous

TRANSPARENCY:
Transparent to
translucent

TESTS:
Uneven, brittle
fracture. White
streak

LOOKALIKES:
Zeolites

Heulandite is a calcium-sodium-rich zeolite,
sometimes with minor barium or strontium.
As with other zeolites it occurs as secondary
infillings in voids, cracks and veins in altered
volcanic rocks. It also occurs in veins in
metamorphic rocks, and in hydrothermal
mineral veins. Found in Scotland, Ireland,
Idar-Oberstein and Harz/Germany,
Kongsberg/Norway, Iceland, France and Italy.
The photograph shows enlargement of small
crystals lining a volcanic cavity.

FAMILY: ZEOLITE

Mesolite • Na_2Ca_2 $Al_6Si_9O_{30}.8H_2O$

Chemical group: Hydrous silicate

ID FACT FILE

CRYSTAL SYSTEM:
Monoclinic

COLOUR:
Colourless, white

WHERE:
Igneous,
metamorphic

ABUNDANCE:
Abundant

FORM:
Long prismatic
crystals, fibrous,
radiating
aggregates

CLEAVAGE:
Perfect

HARDNESS:
5

SG:
2–2.4

LUSTRE:
Vitreous, silky

TRANSPARENCY:
Transparent to
translucent

TESTS:
Conchoidal,
brittle fracture.
White streak

LOOKALIKES:
Zeolites

Mesolite is a zeolite with approximately equal sodium and calcium. It typically forms long slender crystals. As with other zeolites it can also occur as secondary infillings in voids, cracks, gas cavities and veins in altered volcanic rocks. Found in Antrim/Ireland, Faeroes, Iceland, Skye and Mull/Scotland, Auvergne/France.

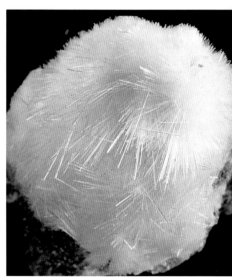

FAMILY: ZEOLITE

Natrolite •
$Na_2Al_2Si_3O_{10}.2H_2O$

Chemical group: Hydrous silicate

ID FACT FILE

CRYSTAL SYSTEM:
Orthorhombic

COLOUR:
White

WHERE:
Igneous,
metamorphic

ABUNDANCE:
Abundant

FORM:
Needle-like
crystals, fibrous,
radiating
aggregates

CLEAVAGE:
Perfect

HARDNESS:
5–5.5

SG:
2.2–2.25

LUSTRE:
Vitreous, pearly

TRANSPARENCY:
Transparent to
translucent

TESTS:
Conchoidal,
brittle fracture.
White streak

LOOKALIKES:
Zeolites

Natrolite is a sodium-rich zeolite that typically forms needle-shaped crystals. As with other zeolites it occurs widely as secondary infillings in voids, cracks and veins in altered volcanic rocks. It also occurs in hydrothermal mineral veins. Found in Antrim/Ireland, Scotland, Idar-Oberstein and Harz/Germany, Iceland, Auvergne/France.

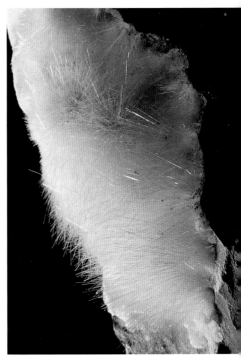

FAMILY: PREHNITE

Prehnite • $Ca_2Al_2Si_3O_{10}.(OH)_2$

Chemical group:Hydrous calcium aluminium silicate

ID FACT FILE

CRYSTAL SYSTEM:
Orthorhombic

COLOUR:
Pale green, white

WHERE:
Metamorphic

ABUNDANCE:
Common

FORM:
Soft white clay;
rarely small
hexagonal
crystals

CLEAVAGE:
Imperfect

HARDNESS:
6–6.5

SG:
2.8–3.0

LUSTRE:
Vitreous, pearly

TRANSPARENCY:
Transparent to
translucent

TESTS:
Uneven fracture.
White streak

LOOKALIKES:
Feldspar

Prehnite forms globular masses with radiating crystal structures in cavities, and also as rare tabular slightly curved crystals. It often has a distinctive pale green colour. It occurs in cavities in igneous lavas often with zeolite minerals. It can be abundant in some metamorphic schists and calc silicate rocks. Found in Idar-Oberstein and Harzburg/Germany, Dauphiné/France, Kilpatrick and Campsie Hills/Scotland.

FAMILY: ZEOLITE

Stilbite • NaCa$_2$Al$_5$Si$_{13}$O$_{36}$.14H$_2$O

Chemical group: Hydrous silicate

ID FACT FILE

CRYSTAL SYSTEM:
Monoclinic

COLOUR:
White, yellowish, reddish

WHERE:
Igneous, metamorphic

ABUNDANCE:
Abundant

FORM:
Thin tabular crystals, radiating sheaf-like aggregates

CLEAVAGE:
Perfect

HARDNESS:
3.5–4

SG:
2.1–2.2

LUSTRE:
Vitreous, pearly

TRANSPARENCY:
Transparent to translucent

TESTS:
Uneven, brittle fracture. White streak

LOOKALIKES:
Zeolites

Stilbite is a sodium- and calcium-rich zeolite that can form characteristic sheaf-like bunches of crystals. As with other zeolites it occurs widely as secondary infillings in voids, cracks and veins in altered volcanic rocks; rather common infilling gas escape cavities in Tertiary basaltic lavas of Antrim/Ireland. It also occurs in hydrothermal mineral veins. Found in Skye and Mull/Scotland, Harz/Germany, Faeroes, Iceland, Auvergne/France, Nova Scotia/Canada.

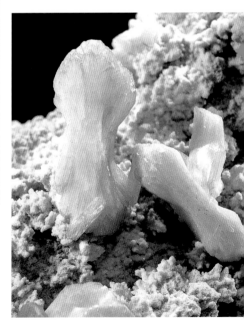

FAMILY: ANDALUSITE

ID FACT FILE

CRYSTAL SYSTEM:
Orthorhombic

COLOUR:
Colourless, grey, reddish

WHERE:
Metamorphic

ABUNDANCE:
Rock-forming

FORM:
Squarish prismatic crystals; also granular, massive

CLEAVAGE:
Poor

HARDNESS:
7.5

SG:
3.1–3.3

LUSTRE:
Vitreous, dull

TRANSPARENCY:
Transparent to opaque

TESTS:
Uneven, brittle fracture. White streak

LOOKALIKES:
Orthoclase

Andalusite • Al_2SiO_5

Chemical group: Alumino-silicate

Andalusite occurs in metamorphic rocks including regional gneiss and schist; it also occurs in contact metamorphic rocks adjacent to high-temperature igneous intrusions. Many cross-sections have a characteristic square shape. The variety *chiastolite* reveals a distinctive internal black cross-like structure set in whitish or grey crystals with squarish outlines. It is found in Cumberland and Cornwall/England and Chile. Impurities can include sodium, potassium and manganese.

FAMILY: BERYL

ID FACT FILE

CRYSTAL SYSTEM:
Hexagonal

COLOUR:
Green, blue, yellow, white

WHERE:
Igneous, metamorphic, sedimentary

ABUNDANCE:
Common

FORM:
Tabular crystals, often twinned; also massive, granular

CLEAVAGE:
Imperfect

HARDNESS:
7.5–8

SG:
2.6–2.9

LUSTRE:
Vitreous

TRANSPARENCY:
Transparent to opaque

TESTS:
Conchoidal, uneven fracture. White streak

LOOKALIKES:
Tourmaline

Beryl • $Be_3Al_2Si_6O_{18}$

Chemical group: Silicate

Beryl in its unattractive cloudy form is the chief source of the element beryllium. It occurs as six-sided prismatic crystals in minor quantities in acid igneous rocks like granite and forms larger prismatic crystals in pegmatite. Precious beryl is beautiful and includes several varieties used for gems. *Emerald* is the famous green variety from pegmatites in Austria, Colombia, Zimbabwe and South Africa. *Aquamarine* is the pale blue variety from pegmatite and granite as in Mourne Mountains/Ireland, Brazil and Madagascar. *Chrysoberyl* is a completely different tabular mineral (Al_2BeO_4) from pegmatites and schists known for the red-green gem variety *alexandrite*.

FAMILY: CHLORITE

Chlorite* • $(Fe,Mg, Mn, Al)_6(Si,Al)_4O_{10}·(OH,O)_8$

Chemical group: Hydrous silicate

ID FACT FILE

CRYSTAL SYSTEM:
Monoclinic

COLOUR:
Green, greenish black

WHERE:
Igneous, metamorphic

ABUNDANCE:
Rock-forming

FORM:
Tabular crystals, granular; scaly aggregates

CLEAVAGE:
Perfect

HARDNESS:
2–3

SG:
2.6–3.4

LUSTRE:
Pearly

TRANSPARENCY:
Translucent to opaque

TESTS:
Flaky fracture. Scratched by fingernail. Grey-green streak

LOOKALIKES:
Actinolite, amphibole

*Chlorite is the name for a group of common, even rock-forming minerals, generally of greenish colour. The important chlorite minerals are the magnesium-iron-rich *chamosite* and *clinochlore,* followed by an oxidised chlorite called *delessite* and a manganese-rich variety *pennantite.* It occurs widely as a secondary mineral in igneous rocks. It is a rock-forming mineral in metamorphic rocks like chlorite-schist.

FAMILY: CHRYSOCOLLA

Chrysocolla • $CuSiO_3.nH_2O$

Chemical group: Hydrous copper silicate

ID FACT FILE

CRYSTAL SYSTEM:
Amorphous

COLOUR:
Bluish green, whitish green, turquoise

WHERE:
Igneous

ABUNDANCE:
Restricted

FORM:
Globular, massive, gel-like

CLEAVAGE:
None

HARDNESS:
2–4

SG:
2–2.2

LUSTRE:
Vitreous, greasy

TRANSPARENCY:
Translucent to opaque

TESTS:
Conchoidal, brittle fracture. White or greenish streak

LOOKALIKES:
Azurite, malachite

Chrysocolla is a distinctive pale to vivid green copper mineral. It contains a variable amount of water, and additional impurities like aluminium. Crystalline forms are unknown, and its apparent lack of internal structure is called amorphous. It commonly occurs in association with other copper minerals in the weathering zone of copper deposits, as in Cornwall and Lake District/England, Urals and Siberia/Russia, Chile, and Zaire.

FAMILY: CORDIERITE

Cordierite • $(Mg,Fe)_2Al_4Si_5O_{18}$

Chemical group: Alumino-silicate

ID FACT FILE

CRYSTAL SYSTEM:
Orthorhombic

COLOUR:
Blue, violet, grey

WHERE:
Metamorphic, igneous

ABUNDANCE:
Rock-forming

FORM:
Crystals rare; massive aggregates

CLEAVAGE:
Imperfect

HARDNESS:
7–7.5

SG:
2.5–2.7

LUSTRE:
Vitreous, greasy

TRANSPARENCY:
Transparent to translucent

TESTS:
Conchoidal, uneven fracture. Bluish white streak

LOOKALIKES:
Andalusite

This alumino-silicate often has a characteristic violet-blue colour but rarely forms distinct crystals. It occurs widely in regional metamorphic rocks, like cordierite-gneiss, and in contact metamorphic rocks like cordierite hornfels; often associated with andalusite. It can also be a minor constituent of some large igneous bodies like norite which have been contaminated by sedimentary rocks.

FAMILY: CHRYSOCOLLA

Dioptase • $CuSiO_2.(OH)_2$

Chemical group: Hydrous copper silicate

ID FACT FILE

CRYSTAL SYSTEM:
Trigonal

COLOUR:
Vivid emerald-green

WHERE:
Igneous

ABUNDANCE:
Uncommon

FORM:
Stubby crystals; rhombic faces

CLEAVAGE:
Perfect

HARDNESS:
5

SG:
3.28–3.35

LUSTRE:
Vitreous

TRANSPARENCY:
Transparent to translucent

TESTS:
Conchoidal, brittle fracture. Green streak

LOOKALIKES:
Unlikely to be mistaken

Dioptase occurs as distinctive emerald-green crystals encrusting surfaces and lining cavities in the weathering zone of copper deposits. It is often associated with copper carbonate minerals and calcite. It is rather uncommon but easily recognised by its colour and well developed rhomb-shaped crystal faces. Found in Kazakhstan/Russia, Arizona/USA, Chile and Zaire.

FAMILY: EPIDOTE

Epidote • $Ca_2(Al, Fe)_3(SiO_4)_3OH$

Chemical group: Silicate

ID FACT FILE

CRYSTAL SYSTEM:
Monoclinic

COLOUR:
Green, yellowish green, black, red°

WHERE:
Metamorphic, igneous

ABUNDANCE:
Rock-forming

FORM:
Prismatic crystals, striated; also granular, massive

CLEAVAGE:
Perfect

HARDNESS:
6–7

SG:
3.3–3.5

LUSTRE:
Vitreous

TRANSPARENCY:
Transparent to opaque

TESTS:
Conchoidal, uneven fracture. Grey streak

LOOKALIKES:
Olivine, augite

Epidote is an abundant and widespread metamorphic mineral occurring in calcium-rich rocks derived from impure limestones or igneous rocks. It also occurs in some igneous rocks like granite. *Clinozoisite* is a pale-coloured variety of epidote that has very little iron; it occurs as a secondary mineral in metamorphosed igneous rocks. *Piemontite°* is a distinctive red variety, with red streak; it has high manganese and occurs in some schists.

FAMILY: HEMIMORPHITE

Hemimorphite • $Zn_4Si_2O_7.(OH)_2.H_2O$

Chemical group: Hydrous zinc silicate

ID FACT FILE

CRYSTAL SYSTEM:
Orthorhombic

COLOUR:
White, brownish,
pale green or
blue

WHERE:
Igneous

ABUNDANCE:
Restricted

FORM:
Small tabular
crystals; also
massive,
globular

CLEAVAGE:
Perfect

HARDNESS:
5

SG:
3.3–3.5

LUSTRE:
Vitreous

TRANSPARENCY:
Transparent to
translucent

TESTS:
Conchoidal,
brittle fracture.
White streak

LOOKALIKES:
Malachite,
chrysocolla

Hemimorphite is a common zinc mineral often with distinctive tabular crystals. It occurs in the weathering or oxidation zone of lead-zinc deposits where it can be accompanied by similar-coloured zinc carbonate (*smithsonite*). It is an important source of zinc. Found in Cumberland and Derbyshire/England, Austria, Russia, Arizona. Uncommon pale green massive forms may be mistaken for green copper minerals, but the presence of any crystals is distinctive.

FAMILY: KAOLINITE

Kaolinite • $Al_2Si_2O_5.(OH)_4$

Chemical group: Hydrous aluminium silicate

ID FACT FILE

CRYSTAL SYSTEM:
Triclinic

COLOUR:
White

WHERE:
Igneous

ABUNDANCE:
Abundant

FORM:
Soft white clay; rarely small hexagonal crystals

CLEAVAGE:
Perfect

HARDNESS:
2–2.5

SG:
2.6

LUSTRE:
Dull

TRANSPARENCY:
Translucent to opaque

TESTS:
Feels greasy. Crumbles to powder

LOOKALIKES:
Other clay minerals

Kaolinite is a white common clay mineral typically formed by alteration of feldspar in granite. It is soft and easily scratched with a fingernail. It may be associated with other minerals like tourmaline and cassiterite in hydrothermally altered granite and greisen. It is locally abundant and even rock-forming; it is extracted for commercial use, as in Cornwall/England and France. The photograph shows kaolinite in the shape of orthoclase crystals; such replacements are called pseudomorphs.

FAMILY: KYANITE

Kyanite • Al_2SiO_5

Chemical group: Alumino-silicate

The blue colour and variation in hardness (hardest across the base of crystals) are distinctive. Kyanite occurs as ruler-like crystals widely distributed in high-grade metamorphic rocks like gneiss, micaschist and eclogite, as in Scotland and Switzerland. Kyanite has the same composition as both sillimanite and andalusite. It can contain impurities of sodium, potassium and chromium.

ID FACT FILE

CRYSTAL SYSTEM:
Orthorhombic

COLOUR:
Light blue, rarely other colours

WHERE:
Metamorphic

ABUNDANCE:
Rock-forming

FORM:
Long bladed crystals

CLEAVAGE:
Poor

HARDNESS:
4–7 (variable)

SG:
3.6–3.7

LUSTRE:
Vitreous, pearly

TRANSPARENCY:
Transparent to translucent

TESTS:
Fibrous, brittle fracture. White streak

LOOKALIKES:
Unlikely to be mistaken

FAMILY: MELILITE

Melilite* • $Ca_2MgSi_2O_7$ to $CaAl_2SiO_7$

Chemical group: Silicate

ID FACT FILE

CRYSTAL SYSTEM:
Tetragonal

COLOUR:
Colourless,
white, grey,
brown

WHERE:
Igneous

ABUNDANCE:
Rock-forming

FORM:
Short prismatic
or tabular
crystals

CLEAVAGE:
Imperfect

HARDNESS:
5–5.5

SG:
2.9–3.1

LUSTRE:
Vitreous to pearly

TRANSPARENCY:
Transparent to
translucent

TESTS:
Uneven, brittle
fracture. White or
grey streak

LOOKALIKES:
Feldspar,
wollastonite

*Melilite is the name for a mineral group with any composition between the pure magnesium *akermanite* and pure aluminium *gehlenite*; it can be either a mafic or a leucocratic mineral. It is an important constituent of alkaline basic igneous rocks like melilite-basalt and nephelinite. Igneous rocks comprised of mostly melilite are called *melilitite* (volcanic) or *melilitolite* (plutonic); they often occur in association with carbonatite. Melilite is a common mineral in chondrite meteorites.

FAMILY: PYROPHYLLITE

Pyrophyllite • $Al_2Si_4O_{10}.(OH)_2$

Chemical group: Hydrous aluminium silicate

ID FACT FILE

CRYSTAL SYSTEM:
Monoclinic

COLOUR:
White, grey, greenish

WHERE:
Metamorphic, igneous

ABUNDANCE:
Common

FORM:
Radiating aggregates, massive; tabular crystals

CLEAVAGE:
Perfect

HARDNESS:
1–1.5

SG:
2.66–2.90

LUSTRE:
Vitreous, pearly

TRANSPARENCY:
Transparent to translucent

TESTS:
Uneven fracture, flexible. White streak. Feels greasy

LOOKALIKES:
Talc

Pyrophyllite is similar in many ways to talc, but can form more distinctive crystalline aggregates, with elongated tabular shapes. It is very soft and easily scratched with a fingernail. It occurs mainly as lenses and beds in metamorphic schists, and also in some hydrothermal mineral veins. Locally rock-forming deposits are mined for industrial use. Found in Eifel/Germany, Belgium, Luxembourg, Finland, North Carolina, Georgia and California/USA and South Africa.

FAMILY: SCAPOLITE

ID FACT FILE

CRYSTAL SYSTEM:
Tetragonal

COLOUR:
Colourless,
white, grey,
brown

WHERE:
Metamorphic

ABUNDANCE:
Abundant

FORM:
Prismatic
crystals; also
massive,
granular

CLEAVAGE:
Perfect

HARDNESS:
5–6.5

SG:
2.54–2.77

LUSTRE:
Vitreous, greasy

TRANSPARENCY:
Transparent to
opaque

TESTS:
Conchoidal,
brittle fracture.
White streak

LOOKALIKES:
Feldspar

Scapolite* •
$3NaAlSi_3O_8.NaCl$ to
$3CaAl_2Si_2O_6.CaCO_3$

Chemical group: Silicate

*Scapolite is the name for a mineral group
with any composition between the pure
sodium *marialite* and pure calcium *meionite*;
common scapolite has a mixed composition
somewhere between these two ideal types. It
is a pale-coloured mineral. It occurs as an
alteration product of plagioclase feldspar in
igneous rocks, but more commonly in
metamorphic rocks like marble, gneiss,
amphibolite and granulite.

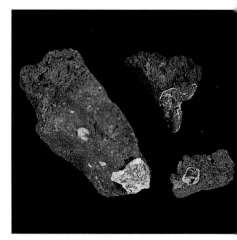

FAMILY: SILLIMANITE

ID FACT FILE

CRYSTAL SYSTEM:
Orthorhombic

COLOUR:
Grey, brownish,
greenish

WHERE:
Metamorphic

ABUNDANCE:
Rock-forming

FORM:
Needle-shaped
crystals,
radiating, fibrous
aggregates

CLEAVAGE:
Perfect

HARDNESS:
3.2–3.3

SG:
6.5–7

LUSTRE:
Vitreous, greasy

TRANSPARENCY:
Transparent to
translucent

TESTS:
Uneven fracture.
White streak

LOOKALIKES:
Rutile

Sillimanite • Al_2SiO_5

Chemical group: Alumino-silicate

Sillimanite is a common alumino-silicate mineral with a very elongated crystal form. It usually occurs as felted aggregates in metamorphic rocks, including contact metamorphosed hornfels. Also occurs widely in regional high-grade metamorphic rocks like gneiss, micaschist, granulite and eclogite as in Finland, Germany, Norway, Scotland and Switzerland. Though it is often abundant, its small grain size can make it difficult to recognise, even with the use of a hand lens.

FAMILY: STAUROLITE

Staurolite • $(Fe,Mg,Zn)_2$ $Al_9(Si,Al)_4O_{22}(OH)_2$

Chemical group: Alumino-silicate

ID FACT FILE

CRYSTAL SYSTEM:
Orthorhombic

COLOUR:
Brown, black

WHERE:
Metamorphic

ABUNDANCE:
Common

FORM:
Stout prismatic crystals, often twinned like a cross or a tilted cross

CLEAVAGE:
Imperfect

HARDNESS:
7–7.5

SG:
3.65–3.77

LUSTRE:
Vitreous

TRANSPARENCY:
Translucent to opaque

TESTS:
Conchoidal fracture. White streak

LOOKALIKES:
Cross unlikely to be mistaken

Staurolite is a metamorphic mineral often associated with kyanite and garnet in aluminium-rich rocks like gneiss and mica-schist. Crystals usually have a dull, rough, slightly pitted surface. Occasionally also occurs as resistant heavy mineral in sedimentary sands. May contain some sodium. The cruciform shape combined with high hardness and dark colour are distinctive features.

FAMILY: TALC

ID FACT FILE

CRYSTAL SYSTEM:
Monoclinic

COLOUR:
Colourless,
white, greenish

WHERE:
Metamorphic

ABUNDANCE:
Rock-forming

FORM:
Massive, scaly,
granular

CLEAVAGE:
Perfect

HARDNESS:
1

SG:
2.7–2.8

LUSTRE:
Pearly, greasy

TRANSPARENCY:
Transparent to
opaque

TESTS:
Flexible. Feels
greasy or soapy.
White streak

LOOKALIKES:
Serpentine

Talc • $Mg_3Si_4O_{10}(OH)_2$

Chemical group: Hydrous magnesium silicate

Talc has distinctive low hardness; it is the
softest mineral in the Moh's scale of hardness
(=1). It has a soapy feel. It occurs in hydrous
altered magnesium-rich igneous rocks like
serpentinite, and in contact metamorphic
zones around granite bodies. It is locally
common in some metamorphosed
limestones, and is a rock-forming mineral in
some schists, as in Germany, Austria,
Scotland and Italy. The photograph is an
enlargement of the scaly form.

FAMILY: TITANITE

ID FACT FILE

CRYSTAL SYSTEM:
Monoclinic

COLOUR:
Brown, yellow, green, black

WHERE:
Igneous

ABUNDANCE:
Common

FORM:
Prismatic crystals, wedge- or lozenge-shaped

CLEAVAGE:
Imperfect

HARDNESS:
5–5.5

SG:
3.4–3.6

LUSTRE:
Greasy

TRANSPARENCY:
Transparent to opaque

TESTS:
Conchoidal, brittle fracture

LOOKALIKES:
Zircon

Titanite • $CaTiSiO_5$

Chemical group: Silicate

Titanite (old name sphene) occurs in small quantities in many coarse-grained igneous rocks like diorite, granite and granodiorite. It is an important host for titanium (Ti), but impurities may also include small amounts of zirconium, lanthanum and cerium. It is distinguished from zircon by its more angular shape and lower hardness.

FAMILY: TOPAZ

ID FACT FILE

CRYSTAL SYSTEM:
Orthorhombic

COLOUR:
Straw-yellow,
brown,
colourless

WHERE:
Igneous

ABUNDANCE:
Common

FORM:
Prismatic
crystals

CLEAVAGE:
Perfect

HARDNESS:
8

SG:
3.5–3.6

LUSTRE:
Vitreous

TRANSPARENCY:
Transparent to
translucent

TESTS:
White streak.
Conchoidal,
uneven fracture

LOOKALIKES:
Zircon

Topaz •
$Ca_2Fe_5Si_8O_{22}(OH)_2$
Chemical group: Silicate

Topaz is a hard mineral that occurs in acid
igneous rocks like granite. It also occurs in
hydrothermal veins with tin minerals, as in
Cornwall/England. Good crystals can be found
protruding into cavities in some granite, as in
Mourne Mountains/Ireland; also in greisen
and especially pegmatite. Uncommon pink or
blue forms are used as gemstones, usually
from sedimentary placer deposits, as in
Urals/Russia and Brazil; colour may be
modified by heating. The photograph shows a
natural crystal and a cut gem.

ID FACT FILE

CRYSTAL SYSTEM:
Tetragonal

COLOUR:
Brown, green, yellow

WHERE:
Igneous, metamorphic, sedimentary

ABUNDANCE:
Rock-forming

FORM:
Equant stubby crystals, often twinned; also massive.

CLEAVAGE:
Poor

HARDNESS:
6.5

SG:
3.3–3.45

LUSTRE:
Vitreous, greasy

TRANSPARENCY:
Transparent to opaque

TESTS:
Uneven, splintery fracture. White streak

LOOKALIKES:
Zircon, melilite

Vesuvianite • $Ca_{10}(Mg, Fe)_2Al_4Si_9O_{34}(OH)_4$

Chemical group: Silicate

Vesuvianite is a complex silicate which occurs widely in metamorphic rocks such as marble, calcium-silicate hornfels and serpentinite; as in Tyrol/Austria, Zermatt/Switzerland, Dolomites/Italy. Often well-formed crystals occur in heat-metamorphosed limestone, as in blocks from Mt Vesuvius/Italy. It is distinguished from zircon by its lower hardness (scratched by quartz), and from melilite by its stubby shape.

FAMILY: ZIRCON

Zircon • ZrSiO$_4$

Chemical group: Silicate

ID FACT FILE

CRYSTAL SYSTEM:
Tetragonal

COLOUR:
Brown, red,
yellow

WHERE:
Igneous,
metamorphic,
sedimentary

ABUNDANCE:
Abundant

FORM:
Stubby prisms,
rounded grains

CLEAVAGE:
Poor

HARDNESS:
7–7.5

SG:
4.7

LUSTRE:
Greasy

TRANSPARENCY:
Transparent to
opaque

TESTS:
White streak.
Conchoidal brittle
fracture

LOOKALIKES:
Topaz

Zircon is the most important source of the element zirconium; it can also contain hafnium. It occurs in small amounts in a wide variety of igneous rocks, from volcanic kimberlite and andesite to coarse-grained granite, nepheline syenite and pegmatite. It also occurs in metamorphic rocks like gneiss. It is resistant to weathering and occurs widely in sedimentary rocks as a 'heavy mineral'; sometimes concentrated in beach sands and mined, as in Australia and Brazil. The photograph shows a group of collected crystals, much enlarged.

FAMILY: EPIDOTE

Zoisite •
$Ca_2Al_3(SiO_4)_3OH$

Chemical group: Silicate

ID FACT FILE

CRYSTAL SYSTEM:
Orthorhombic

COLOUR:
White, grey,
green, blue,
pink°

WHERE:
Metamorphic

ABUNDANCE:
Abundant

FORM:
Prismatic,
striated crystals;
massive
aggregates

CLEAVAGE:
Perfect

HARDNESS:
6–6.5

SG:
3.2–3.37

LUSTRE:
Vitreous

TRANSPARENCY:
Transparent to
opaque

TESTS:
Conchoidal,
splintery fracture.
White streak

LOOKALIKES:
Pyroxene,
wollastonite

Zoisite is an alumino-silicate that occurs commonly in metamorphic rocks derived from igneous rocks with calcium-rich feldspar, like amphibolite. Impurities can include manganese which gives a rose-pink colour in the variety *thulite*. *Tanzanite* is a distinctive blue colour and is used as a gemstone; it is only known from gneisses in northern Tanzania.

FAMILY: AXINITE

Axinite • (Ca,Mn,Fe) $Al_2BSi_4O_{15}(OH)$

Chemical group: Boro-silicate

ID FACT FILE

CRYSTAL SYSTEM:
Triclinic

COLOUR:
Brown, grey, violet, green

WHERE:
Metamorphic, igneous

ABUNDANCE:
Common

FORM:
Tabular or wedge-shaped crystals

CLEAVAGE:
Perfect

HARDNESS:
6.5–7

SG:
3.3–3.4

LUSTRE:
3.3–3.4

TRANSPARENCY:
Transparent to translucent

TESTS:
Choncoidal, brittle fracture. White streak

LOOKALIKES:
Titanite

Axinite is a silicate with essential boron (B), a boro-silicate. It usually forms thin and very sharp edged, axe-like crystals. It occurs in contact metamorphic rocks around granites and in cavities within granite, as in Cornwall/England. It may be associated with other boro-silicate minerals like tourmaline. It also occurs in calc silicate hornfels as in Harz/Germany and Dauphiné/France.

FAMILY: GADOLINITE

ID FACT FILE

CRYSTAL SYSTEM:
Monoclinic

COLOUR:
Colourless, pale
yellow or green

WHERE:
Igneous,
metamorphic

ABUNDANCE:
Restricted

FORM:
Stubby prismatic
or tabular
crystals; massive

CLEAVAGE:
None

HARDNESS:
5–5.5

SG:
2.9–3.0

LUSTRE:
Vitreous, greasy

TRANSPARENCY:
Transparent to
translucent

TESTS:
Conchoidal
fracture. White
streak

LOOKALIKES:
Wollastonite

Datolite • CaBSiO$_4$OH

Chemical group: Boro-silicate

Datolite is a boro-silicate with simple
composition and a pale colour. It is related to
the gadolinite group of minerals, which are
characterised by their high concentrations of
rare earth elements; some cerium and
lanthanum can occur as impurities in datolite.
It occurs in small quantities in basic igneous
rocks, pegmatites and in metamorphic rocks.
Found in Harz/Germany, Arendal/Norway,
and Massachusetts and New Jersey and USA.

FAMILY: TOURMALINE

Tourmaline • (Na,Ca) $(Li,Mg,Fe,Al)_3(Al,Fe)_6$ $B_3Si_6O_{27}(O,OH,F)_4$

Chemical group: Boro-silicate

ID FACT FILE

CRYSTAL SYSTEM:
Trigonal

COLOUR:
Black, blue; all colours

WHERE:
Igneous, metamorphic

ABUNDANCE:
Rock-forming

FORM:
Elongated prismatic crystals; also radiating, granular

CLEAVAGE:
None

HARDNESS:
7–7.5

SG:
3–3.2

LUSTRE:
Vitreous

TRANSPARENCY:
Transparent to opaque

TESTS:
Choncoidal, uneven fracture. White streak. Striated crystals, triangular cross sections

LOOKALIKES:
Apatite

Tourmaline is a boro-silicate with variable composition. It occurs in small quantities in acid igneous rocks like granite, and is locally abundant or rock-forming. It also occurs in small quantities in many metamorphic rocks, like gneiss and mica-schist; also in sedimentary placer deposits. *Schorl* is an iron-rich black or blue variety. *Elbaite* is lithium-rich tourmaline, often pink or green. *Dravite* is magnesium-rich, yellow or brown. *Rubellite* is the name for the rose-pink variety often used as a semiprecious gem.

FAMILY: BORATE

ID FACT FILE

CRYSTAL SYSTEM:
Monoclinic

COLOUR:
White

WHERE:
Sedimentary,
salt lakes

ABUNDANCE:
Restricted

FORM:
Prismatic
crystals; also
massive

CLEAVAGE:
Good cleavage in
two directions

HARDNESS:
2–2.5

SG:
1.7

LUSTRE:
Vitreous

TRANSPARENCY:
Translucent

TESTS:
White streak.
Tastes sweet or
alkaline (test not
recommended)

LOOKALIKES:
Colemanite and
other borate

Borax • $Na_2B_4O_7.10H_2O$

Chemical group: Borate

Borax is the best-known borate mineral and has
a distinctive crystal form and low SG. It occurs
in desiccated salt lakes, playas or borax marshes
together with other borates such as *colemanite*,
as in California/USA. Borates, including borax,
may also form as hydrothermal deposits from
volcanic hot springs.

FAMILY: FOSSIL RESIN

Amber •
$C_{10}H_{16}O$ (variable)

Chemical group: Succinic acid

ID FACT FILE

CRYSTAL SYSTEM:
Amorphous

COLOUR:
Orangy yellow to brown

WHERE:
Sedimentary

ABUNDANCE:
Restricted

FORM:
Nodular

CLEAVAGE:
None

HARDNESS:
2–2.5

SG:
1.1–1.3

LUSTRE:
Greasy, resinous

TRANSPARENCY:
Transparent to opaque

TESTS:
Conchoidal fracture. White streak

LOOKALIKES:
Unlikely to be mistaken

Amber is a fossil resin that is frequently clouded and can contain fossil insects or parts of plant debris; it is the fossilised resin from pine trees. It occurs in young sedimentary rocks of estuarine origin or beach deposits. Found in countries around the Baltic Sea, Romania, Siberia.

FAMILY: LIGNITE COAL

Jet • C,H,N,O (variable)

Chemical group: Carbon-rich

ID FACT FILE

CRYSTAL SYSTEM:
Amorphous

COLOUR:
Very black

WHERE:
Sedimentary

ABUNDANCE:
Restricted

FORM:
Nodular, even-coloured lumps

CLEAVAGE:
None

HARDNESS:
1.5–2.5

SG:
1.2

LUSTRE:
Brilliant, resinous

TRANSPARENCY:
Opaque

TESTS:
Conchoidal fracture. Brown to black streak. Takes a good polish

LOOKALIKES:
Coals

Jet is an intense black coloured variety of lignite or brown coal that takes a very high polish and is used for ornaments, as at Whitby/Yorkshire/England. Jet was also known to the Greeks from Asia Minor. Lignite occurs in coal-bearing sedimentary strata, and has a brilliant lustre; often contains fossil plant remains. Found in England, Germany and Hungary.

Andesite

Chemical group: Intermediate igneous

Named for the Andes in South America, where it is abundant, andesite is intermediate in composition between basalt and rhyolite. The rock texture is characterised by two grain sizes (*porphyritic*); large crystals of plagioclase, sometimes angular and broken, and several mafic crystals are set in a 'basaltic' or glassy matrix. The mafic minerals can include any or all of olivine, hornblende, biotite and pyroxenes. It is the characteristic product of volcanoes related to subduction as around the Pacific rim.

FAMILY: GRANITE

ID FACT FILE

ESSENTIAL MINERALS:
Alkali feldspar,
plagioclase,
quartz

OTHER MINERALS:
Biotite,
hornblende,
muscovite,
biotite,
tourmaline,
apatite

MINERAL PROPORTIONS:
Alkali feldspar>
plagioclase>
quartz

COLOUR:
Light-coloured,
pinkish, reddish.
Distinctive
texture

TEXTURAL FEATURES:
Even-textured
rock, small
granular crystals,
sugary texture

DISTRIBUTION:
Related to large
granites

ABUNDANCE:
Widespread

LOOKALIKES:
Pelsite

Aplite

Chemical group: Acid igneous

Aplite is a fine-grained variety of granite with a granular sugary texture. It occurs as small bodies, dykes or veins, associated with large masses of coarse-grained granite, or pegmatites, especially near the edges of large intrusions. Occasionally aplites can be found in rock types other than granite, such as syenite. A fine-grained granite with much less quartz and more feldspar called *felsite* can also occur.

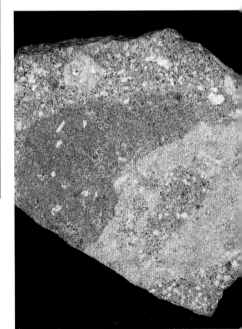

Basalt

Chemical group: Basic igneous

ID FACT FILE

ESSENTIAL MINERALS:
Plagioclase, augite

OTHER MINERALS:
Olivine, pyroxenes, spinel, ilmenite, magnetite, apatite

MINERAL PROPORTIONS:
Plagioclase> augite

COLOUR:
Black, very dark grey; paler and greenish if altered

TEXTURAL FEATURES:
Usually larger crystals (phenocrysts) set in finely crystalline matrix, which may have vesicles and occasionally glass

DISTRIBUTION:
Oceanic islands, continental volcanoes, flood plateau lavas

ABUNDANCE:
Widespread; constitutes all seafloor crust

LOOKALIKES:
Glassy volcanic rocks

Basalt is a finely crystalline igneous rock, which is sometimes glassy, and represents rapidly cooled magma derived from the Earth's upper mantle. It is recognised primarily by its very dark colour. It may contain visible larger crystals of olivine (olivine basalt; *see* p.164), pyroxene or plagioclase. It is the most widely distributed volcanic rock. Molten basaltic magma is very fluid and can form vast lava flows, as well as pillows. When cooled more slowly it forms dolerite or gabbro (*see* p.180 and p.183). Found at Antrim/Ireland, Skye and Mull/Scotland, Iceland, Auvergne/France, Germany, Italy and most countries.

FAMILY: BASALT

ID FACT FILE

ESSENTIAL MINERALS:
Plagioclase, augite, olivine

OTHER MINERALS:
Pyroxenes, spinel, ilmenite, magnetite, apatite

MINERAL PROPORTIONS:
Plagioclase> augite>olivine

COLOUR:
Black, very dark grey; prominent green olivine crystals

TEXTURAL FEATURES:
Large olivine crystals (phenocrysts) set in finely crystalline matrix, which may have vesicles and occasionally glass

DISTRIBUTION:
Oceanic islands, continental volcanoes

ABUNDANCE:
Widespread

LOOKALIKES:
Unlikely to be mistaken

Olivine Basalt

Chemical group: Basic igneous

Olivine basalt is a variety of basalt (*see* p.163). Larger crystals of olivine are distinctive rounded or stubby prisms. Varieties particularly rich in olivine may be called *picrite*. Two further varieties which have large crystals of both green olivine and black augite, as well as abundant rounded holes after volcanic gas, are known as *oceanite* (with just a little augite) and *ankaramite* (with approximately equal amounts of olivine and augite).

FAMILY: DACITE

ID FACT FILE

ESSENTIAL MINERALS:
Plagioclase,
quartz,
hornblende/
biotite/pyroxene

OTHER MINERALS:
Alkali feldspar,
magnetite,
apatite

MINERAL PROPORTIONS:
Plagioclase>
quartz

COLOUR:
Pale grey,
pinkish,
greenish.
Distinctive
texture

TEXTURAL FEATURES:
Large crystals
(phenocrysts)
including
plagioclase
always present;
set in finely
crystalline or
glassy matrix,
which may have
vesicles and
often shows a
good flow texture

DISTRIBUTION:
Related to
subduction,
island arcs,
calderas

ABUNDANCE:
Widespread

LOOKALIKES:
Andesite

Dacite

Chemical group: Intermediate igneous

Dacite is named after a province in Romania. It is intermediate to acidic in composition, between andesite and rhyolite. The rock texture is characterised by two grain sizes (porphyritic); large crystals of plagioclase and quartz, sometimes angular and broken, and mafic crystals are set in a 'basaltic' or glassy matrix. The mafic minerals are pyroxene, hornblende or biotite. Olivine absent, and more quartz than andesite.

FAMILY: GRANITE/DACITE

ID FACT FILE

ESSENTIAL MINERALS:
Alkali feldspar,
plagioclase,
quartz

OTHER MINERALS:
Hornblende,
mica, pyroxene,
magnetite, glass,
kaolinite

MINERAL PROPORTIONS:
Mostly alkali
feldspar

COLOUR:
Pinkish, reddish,
brownish
coloured

TEXTURAL FEATURES:
Irregular volcanic
texture (see tuff;
p.175), glassy
shards, many
gas voids

DISTRIBUTION:
Occurs in vast
sheets
associated with
large calderas

ABUNDANCE:
Widespread

LOOKALIKES:
Tuff

Ignimbrite
Chemical group: Acid igneous

Ignimbrite is a silica-rich igneous rock
occurring in large sheet-like bodies which
partly resemble lava flows. It is formed from
violent eruptions of dacite or rhyolite magma
during catastrophic caldera collapse.
Ignimbrites represent products of the largest
known volcanic eruptions on Earth and may
extend over tens or even hundreds of
kilometres. They contain concentrations of
pumice and distinctive flame-like shattered
glass fragments; they show cooling joints like
lavas. They are associated with andesite, dacite
and rhyolite volcanism, as in the Andes/South
America, New Zealand, Oregon and
Montana/USA, and with Pacific rim volcanism;
they also occur in oceanic islands, as at
Tenerife/Canary Islands. Older ignimbrites
have infilled voids and are harder, as in
Snowdonia/Wales and Lake District/England.

Komatiite

Chemical group: Basic/ultrabasic igneous

ID FACT FILE

ESSENTIAL MINERALS:
Olivine,
pyroxene, glass

OTHER MINERALS:
Plagioclase,
spinel,
serpentine,
amphibole,
chlorite

MINERAL PROPORTIONS:
Olivine or
pyroxene
dominant

COLOUR:
Dark-coloured,
greenish.
Distinctive
texture

TEXTURAL FEATURES:
Large elongated
feathery crystals
set in finely
crystalline,
feathery or
glassy matrix
(spinifex texture)

DISTRIBUTION:
Related to
metamorphic
'greenstone
belts' in very old
crust and rarely
in some younger
igneous flood
basalt provinces

ABUNDANCE:
Common

LOOKALIKES:
Texture unlikely
to be mistaken

Komatiites are rapidly-cooled volcanic lavas formed from volcanic eruptions of the hottest magmas known on Earth (perhaps 1500–1600°C/2730–2910°F). They are associated with substantial sulphide ore deposits for nickel and other metals, sometimes including gold and platinum. Found at Barberton/South Africa, Zimbabwe, Australia, Abitibi/Canada, Finland and India. The youngest komatiites (approximately 60 million years old) occur in Isla Gorgona/Colombia.

FAMILY: VOLCANIC

ID FACT FILE

ESSENTIAL MINERALS:
Glass

OTHER MINERALS:
Alkali feldspar, quartz

MINERAL PROPORTIONS:
Mostly glass

COLOUR:
Black, dark colours; some white features

TEXTURAL FEATURES:
Massive glass with conchoidal fracture; thin flakes transparent

DISTRIBUTION:
Relatively young volcanic

ABUNDANCE:
Locally common

LOOKALIKES:
Unlikely to be mistaken

Obsidian

Chemical group: Intermediate/acid igneous

Obsidian is a silica-rich natural glass, associated with relatively young lava flows. It has a distinctive glassy nature, with conchoidal fracture and very sharp edges; its use for knives and arrows makes it an important archaeological material. Obsidian occurs as crusts on lavas, as complete flows or as near-surface volcanic domes. It is usually of rhyolite composition and forms by slow flow of very viscous lava; other obsidian compositions include phonolite, andesite and trachyte. Found at Iceland, Anatolia/Turkey, Lipari/Italy, Hungary, New Mexico and Wyoming/USA, Japan. *Pitchstone* is a resinous variety of natural volcanic glass, developed by ageing; it has more crystals similar to rhyolite and occurs in older volcanic and igneous rocks, as in Eigg and Arran/Scotland, Saxony/Germany, S Tyrol/Italy, Colorado/USA.

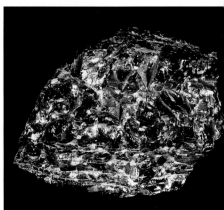

ID FACT FILE

ESSENTIAL MINERALS:
Alkali feldspar, nepheline, pyroxene

OTHER MINERALS:
Amphibole, melanite, olivine, magnetite, apatite, glass

MINERAL PROPORTIONS:
Feldspar> nepheline> pyroxene

COLOUR:
Grey, greenish, brownish

TEXTURAL FEATURES:
Large crystals of feldspar and nepheline in a fine-grained matrix, which may be glassy

DISTRIBUTION:
Continental rifts, alkaline volcanism

ABUNDANCE:
Common

LOOKALIKES:
Basalt

Phonolite

Chemical group: Alkaline igneous

Phonolite is an alkaline igneous rock with characteristic blocky or tabular feldspar (sanidine/anorthoclase), squarish nepheline crystals and black pyroxene (aegirine-augite). It is the fine-grained equivalent to nepheline syenite. It occurs primarily as lava flows but also as small subvolcanic bodies; thicker bodies show columnar jointing. Phonolites occur in huge quantities in some thick continental lava piles, as in the East African Rift Valley. Found at Kaiserstuhl/Germany, Auvergne/France, Devon/England, Montana/USA.

ID FACT FILE

ESSENTIAL MINERALS:
Alkali feldspar, plagioclase, quartz

OTHER MINERALS:
Pyroxene, amphibole, zircon, magnetite, apatite

MINERAL PROPORTIONS:
Mostly feldspars and quartz

COLOUR:
Pale grey, reddish, brownish; darker when old

TEXTURAL FEATURES:
Fine-grained rock, often glassy with larger quartz and feldspar crystals

DISTRIBUTION:
Related to subduction, continental volcanoes, calderas

ABUNDANCE:
Common

LOOKALIKES:
Trachyte

Rhyolite

Chemical group: Acid igneous

Rhyolite is a fine-grained volcanic equivalent to granite. It is the most silica-rich volcanic rock (>66% SiO_2) and forms thick viscous lobate lava flows and volcanic domes, sometimes with columnar cooling joints. It often shows prominent parallel banding with different shades of colour produced during flow. In young volcanoes it is often glassy and may be vesicular; older rhyolites are darker, partly due to staining from iron minerals and alteration of glass. Found at Lake District/England, Snowdonia/Wales, Iceland, Vosges/France, Saxony/Germany, Lipari and Tuscany/Italy, Andes/South America.

FAMILY: TEPHRITE

ID FACT FILE

ESSENTIAL MINERALS:
Feldspathoid,
pyroxene,
hornblende,
plagioclase,
alkali feldspar

OTHER MINERALS:
Olivine,
magnetite,
analcime, apatite

MINERAL PROPORTIONS:
Variable, but
similar amounts
of dark/light
minerals;
prominent
feldspathoids

COLOUR:
Dark grey,
greenish,
brownish; mottled
appearance

TEXTURAL FEATURES:
Large crystals of
nepheline or
leucite with
pyroxene and
hornblende in a
basalt-like or
glassy matrix; gas
voids common

DISTRIBUTION:
Related to
alkaline
volcanism in
continental rifts
or oceanic
islands

ABUNDANCE:
Common

LOOKALIKES:
Basalt lacks
prominent
feldspathoids

Tephrite
Chemical group: Basic/alkaline igneous

Tephrite is a basalt-like lava but with prominent feldspathoids, nepheline and/or leucite, together with pyroxene (augite) and hornblende in a fine-grained or glassy matrix. Voids caused by volcanic gas may be lined with zeolites. It occurs as lava flows associated with relatively young alkaline volcanoes. Found at Vesuvius/Italy, Auvergne/France, Eifel and Kaiserstuhl/Germany. *Basanite* is a variety of tephrite that has olivine and less feldspathoid and is more similar to basalt; found at Canary Islands, Eifel/Germany, Ayrshire/Scotland. *Limburgite* is a variety with mostly glass.

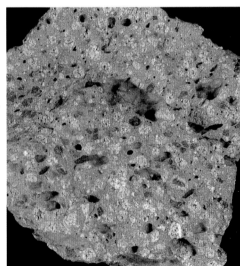

ID FACT FILE

ESSENTIAL MINERALS:
Alkali feldspar, nepheline or quartz

OTHER MINERALS:
Pyroxene, amphibole, melanite, magnetite, apatite

MINERAL PROPORTIONS:
Mostly alkali feldspar. Feldspar> nepheline> pyroxene

COLOUR:
Pale grey, pinkish, brownish

TEXTURAL FEATURES:
Fine-grained rock with few dark crystals

DISTRIBUTION:
Continental rifts, alkaline volcanism

ABUNDANCE:
Common

LOOKALIKES:
Phonolite, rhyolite

Trachyte

Chemical group: Alkaline igneous

Trachyte is a fine-grained, pale-coloured, alkaline igneous rock, made mostly of alkali feldspar (sanidine/anorthoclase). It is the fine-grained equivalent of plutonic syenite. It occurs primarily as lava flows but also as small subvolcanic bodies; thicker bodies show columnar jointing. It often occurs in association with phonolites as in the East African Rift Valley. Found at Devon/England, Westerwald/Germany, North Wales, Auvergne/France, Colorado/USA.

FAMILY: VOLCANIC DEPOSITS

ID FACT FILE

ESSENTIAL MINERALS:
Basaltic minerals plus glass (or altered glass)

OTHER MINERALS:
None

MINERAL PROPORTIONS:
Similar to basalt; glass often replaced by chlorite/clays

COLOUR:
Black; dark grey, reddish or greenish when old

TEXTURAL FEATURES:
Characteristic shapes, gas voids, radial cooling joints, external glassy margin

DISTRIBUTION:
Basaltic lavas which flow into water; oceanic islands, seafloor

ABUNDANCE:
Abundant

LOOKALIKES:
Unlikely to be mistaken

Pillow lava

Chemical group: Basic igneous

Volcanic pillows form when lava flows, usually basaltic, enter water, as at submarine eruptions along ocean ridges forming a continuous layer of all seafloors, and locally at oceanic islands, eg Hawaii, Iceland, Canary Islands. The rapid chilling produces a glassy margin, radial cooling joints and concentric distribution of gas voids concentrated towards the rim. Pillows are head-sized to pillow-sized and have rounded shapes, often with downward-pointing tongues between successively accumulated pillows. The gas voids frequently become filled with secondary minerals such as zeolites and calcite. Old pillows are commonly found in uplifted relics of seafloor (ophiolite), as at Southern Uplands/Scotland and Cyprus.

FAMILY: VOLCANIC DEPOSITS

ID FACT FILE

ESSENTIAL MINERALS:
Mostly glass

OTHER MINERALS:
None

MINERAL PROPORTIONS:
Very few if any minerals

COLOUR:
Pale grey, cream, white, greenish

TEXTURAL FEATURES:
Frothy texture of gas voids and glass, sometimes lacy

DISTRIBUTION:
Generally restricted to silica-rich volcanoes

ABUNDANCE:
Common

LOOKALIKES:
Unlikely to be mistaken

Pumice

Chemical group: Intermediate/acid igneous

Pumice is formed quickly as a mixture of expanding volcanic gas and magma. The resulting frothy texture superficially resembles a sponge, but the pores are not connected; hence pumice floats on water. It occurs in silica-rich volcanoes during violent eruptions of gas-rich magma, like dacite and rhyolite. The glass alters to clay minerals, producing the whitish colours and rather soft pumice. Occurs with bedded tuffs or ignimbrites, as at Santorini/Greece, Lipari and Naples/Italy, Iceland, Auvergne/France, Canary Islands, Andes/South America. *Scoria* is less frothy, denser glass that occurs in basaltic or alkaline volcanoes and is usually reddish.

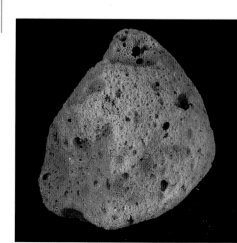

FAMILY: VOLCANIC DEPOSITS

Tuff

Chemical group: All igneous

ID FACT FILE

ESSENTIAL MINERALS:
Any rock-forming minerals

OTHER MINERALS:
Glass, old rock fragments

MINERAL PROPORTIONS:
Any

COLOUR:
Brown, grey, yellow, red

TEXTURAL FEATURES:
Bedded, porous, loose, uncemented; highly variable

DISTRIBUTION:
All young volcanoes; especially andesites and acid igneous varieties

ABUNDANCE:
Abundant

LOOKALIKES:
Uncemented sediments

Volcanic tuff is the general term for all uncemented or loose deposits of volcanoes, also known as pyroclastic rocks. These grade into genuine sedimentary rocks. The composition reflects the general parent magma and igneous rock type of the source volcano. Tuffs are subdivided according to grain size; *ash* is the finest (<2 mm), *lapilli* are small pea-sized pebbles (2–64 mm), and *blocks* and *bombs* are the largest (>64 mm, commonly up to metre-scale sizes). Coarse materials are only found close to the volcano, while finer materials are more widely dispersed. Blocks are usually solidified magma broken from vents, lavas or domes. Volcanic bombs are formed from hot lava blobs that are chilled during passage through the air (*see* p.176). Cemented or heat-welded varieties of tuff include ignimbrite (*see* p.166).

Volcanic bomb

Chemical group: Most igneous

Volcanic bombs are distinctive forms of solidified lava, usually with crystals, formed from ejected blobs of hot lava which rapidly cool when thrown through the air. They tend to rotate during flight, resulting in twisted, spindle-like or contorted shapes. Usually solid before impact, they sometimes bend, and some are modified by rolling down slopes; gas-rich lava bombs may continue to expand slightly resulting in *breadcrust* forms. Often black and glassy when freshly formed, they rapidly change to a reddish colour due to iron oxides. Found at Vesuvius, Etna and Stromboli/Italy, Iceland, Canary Islands, Massif Central/France, Hawaii.

FAMILY: GABBRO

Anorthosite

Chemical group: Ultrabasic igneous

ID FACT FILE

ESSENTIAL MINERALS:
Plagioclase

OTHER MINERALS:
Pyroxenes, olivine, spinel, ilmenite, magnetite, biotite, apatite

MINERAL PROPORTIONS:
Plagioclase makes up >90%

COLOUR:
White, pale grey

TEXTURAL FEATURES:
Granitic texture, crystals intergrown; may show alignment of platy feldspars or layering

DISTRIBUTION:
Deeper continental crust eg Norway, Labrador and Quebec/Canada, South Africa

ABUNDANCE:
Locally abundant but much less common than gabbro

LOOKALIKES:
Unlikely to be mistaken

Anorthosite is a very plagioclase-rich variety of the gabbro family. The plagioclase is almost pure anorthite in composition, giving the rock a low silica content and ultrabasic composition (SiO_2 < wt.%). The dark minerals, which are chiefly pyroxenes, olivine and spinel, make up less than 10 per cent of the rock. It occurs as discrete layers in some large ultrabasic intrusions, as at Rhum and Skye/Scotland. The photograph illustrates centimetre-scale bands of pure anorthosite alternating with thin dark layers richer in pyroxene and olivine: a layered anorthosite. Smashed anorthosite (breccia) forms the highly reflective bright surface of parts of the Moon.

FAMILY: CARBONATITE

ID FACT FILE

ESSENTIAL MINERALS:
Calcite, dolomite

OTHER MINERALS:
Forsterite, diopside, mica, magnetite, siderite, apatite, melanite, melilite, barite, pyrochlore and rare minerals

MINERAL PROPORTIONS:
Mostly carbonates

COLOUR:
White, pale-coloured

TEXTURAL FEATURES:
Coarse-grained interlocking carbonate crystals, few dark minerals

DISTRIBUTION:
Occurs in large igneous masses and as volcanic rocks

ABUNDANCE:
Restricted

LOOKALIKES:
Marble

Carbonatite

Chemical group: Alkaline igneous

Carbonatite is a rare but distinctive rock whose carbonate minerals 'fizz' with dilute acid. It occurs in association with alkaline igneous rocks, such as plutonic nepheline syenite and ijolite and volcanic nephelinite and melilitite. Currently only one volcano erupts carbonatite magma: Oldoinyo Lengai in Tanzania. Carbonatites are found in continental rifts or grabens as in East Africa, Kaiserstuhl/Germany and Oslo/Norway. Old carbonatites are mined for niobium, tantalum and rare earth minerals, as in Finland, Brazil, South Africa and Kola/Russia.

FAMILY: DIORITE

ID FACT FILE

ESSENTIAL MINERALS:
Plagioclase, hornblende, biotite

OTHER MINERALS:
Quartz, augite, magnetite, alkali feldspar, apatite, chlorite

MINERAL PROPORTIONS:
Mostly plagioclase

COLOUR:
Light to dark grey, greenish

TEXTURAL FEATURES:
Medium- to fine-grained with interlocking crystals, sometimes porphyritic with scattered larger crystals

DISTRIBUTION:
Occurs in small intrusive igneous bodies, sometimes near the edges of granites

ABUNDANCE:
Locally common

LOOKALIKES:
Gabbro, dolerite

Diorite

Chemical group: Intermediate igneous

Diorite is a fine- to medium-grained completely crystalline igneous rock with no glass and no void spaces. It is used as ornamental material as it takes a good polish. Darker varieties contain more hornblende, augite or biotite and can appear very similar to gabbro or dolerite, though the presence of some biotite is usually diagnostic. Altered varieties often contain chlorite. Found in Argyll/Scotland, Jersey/Channel Islands, Harz/Germany, Finland, Washington/ USA. Varieties with golf-ball sized round 'bull's eyes' of minerals are known as orbicular diorites, as in Corsica/France and Finland. Below: microscopic view of thin section.

FAMILY: BASALT

ID FACT FILE

ESSENTIAL MINERALS:
Plagioclase,
augite

OTHER MINERALS:
Olivine,
hornblende,
biotite, quartz,
magnetite,
ilmenite, alkali
feldspar, apatite

MINERAL PROPORTIONS:
Plagioclase>
augite

COLOUR:
Dark medium
grey. Distinctive
texture

TEXTURAL FEATURES:
Medium-grained
variety of basalt,
with easily
distinguished
'spiky' white
plagioclase set
in dark mineral
matrix, mostly
pyroxene; entirely
crystalline, no
glass but may
have vesicles

DISTRIBUTION:
Common variety
of subvolcanic
basalt, in minor
intrusions like
dykes and sills

ABUNDANCE:
Widespread

LOOKALIKES:
Basalt, gabbro

Dolerite

Chemical group: Basic igneous

Dolerite is the medium-grained variety of
basalt that is not as coarse-grained as gabbro. It
typically occurs as dykes and sills, as in the
Whin sill in the North of England, which
displays prominent columnar cooling joints. In
addition to pyroxene (augite), dolerite may
contain some olivine or quartz (not both) and a
variety of less abundant minerals. When
altered, it often takes a greenish colour due to
the presence of chlorite minerals. The texture
observable with a hand lens shows small white
plagioclases surrounded by larger dark augite,
with random orientation.

FAMILY: PERIDOTITE

ID FACT FILE

ESSENTIAL MINERALS:
Olivine

OTHER MINERALS:
Chromite,
pyroxene, mica

MINERAL PROPORTIONS:
More than 90%
olivine

COLOUR:
Green when
fresh

TEXTURAL FEATURES:
Distinctive
olivine, granular

DISTRIBUTION:
Occurs in uplifted
mantle rocks, in
large basic
intrusions

ABUNDANCE:
Restricted

LOOKALIKES:
Peridotite

Dunite

Chemical group: Ultrabasic igneous

Dunite is a rock composed almost entirely of
one mineral, olivine (forsterite), and reflects
the colour of olivine. When altered, it can be
replaced by serpentine, which may be reddish.
It occurs in large masses of metamorphosed
olivine-rich rocks like peridotite and
serpentinite; it also occurs in association with
other ultramafic igneous rocks, such as
plutonic pyroxenite and volcanic komatiite.
Found in Aheim/Norway, Troödos/Cyprus,
Mount Dun/New Zealand, South Africa.

ID FACT FILE

ESSENTIAL MINERALS:
Plagioclase,
pyroxene,
hornblende

OTHER MINERALS:
Biotite,
feldspathoids,
ilmenite,
magnetite,
apatite, titanite

MINERAL PROPORTIONS:
Similar amounts
of light
(feldspars) and
dark minerals

COLOUR:
Dark grey;
mottled

TEXTURAL FEATURES:
Granitic texture,
crystals
intergrown;
sometimes
porphyritic

DISTRIBUTION:
Continental
crust, associated
with alkaline
igneous rocks

ABUNDANCE:
Uncommon

LOOKALIKES:
Gabbro

Essexite

Chemical group: Basic igneous

Essexite is a variety of gabbro with a higher
total content of dark minerals, including
titanium-bearing pyroxene and hornblende. It
often includes small amounts of feldspathoids,
such as nepheline and analcime. Its texture is
medium- to coarse-grained as for gabbro (*see*
p.183). It forms only small bodies, as at S
Tyrol/Italy, the east coast of Scotland and in
the Rhine graben at Kaiserstuhl/Germany. A
variety of gabbro similar to essexite but with
more nepheline is *theralite*, as found in
Scotland and Auvergne/France.

FAMILY: GABBRO

ID FACT FILE

ESSENTIAL MINERALS:
Plagioclase,
pyroxenes

OTHER MINERALS:
Olivine,
hornblende,
spinel, ilmenite,
magnetite,
apatite

MINERAL PROPORTIONS:
Plagioclase>
augite

COLOUR:
Dark grey,
greenish,
brownish

TEXTURAL FEATURES:
Granitic texture,
crystals
intergrown; may
show alignment
of platy
feldspars, or
layering

DISTRIBUTION:
Deeper
continental crust;
uplifted oceanic
crust

ABUNDANCE:
Widespread

LOOKALIKES:
Dolerite, diorite

Gabbro

Chemical group: Basic igneous

Gabbro is the coarsely crystalline equivalent of basalt, and results from complete slow crystallisation at depth in the crust. It is a dark-coloured rock, with strongly intergrown minerals, making it tough. The major dark minerals are pyroxene, olivine and hornblende. The pyroxene can include both augite and enstatite-hypersthene. The plagioclase is close to anorthite in composition. Varieties of gabbro include olivine-rich *troctolite* (*see* p.197), hypersthene-rich *norite* (*see* p.192) and nearly pure plagioclase rock called *anorthosite* (*see* p.177).

FAMILY: GRANITE

ID FACT FILE

ESSENTIAL MINERALS:
Alkali feldspar,
plagioclase,
quartz

OTHER MINERALS:
Biotite,
hornblende,
augite,
muscovite,
apatite, zircon,
magnetite

**MINERAL
PROPORTIONS:**
Alkali feldspar>
plagioclase>
quartz. These 3
minerals make
up more than
80% of the rock

COLOUR:
Mottled, grey,
pink or yellowish

TEXTURAL FEATURES:
Coarse-grained
interlocking
crystals;
granular. Quartz
forms irregular
shapes between
feldspars (but
see Varieties,
opposite)

DISTRIBUTION:
Continental crust
of all ages

ABUNDANCE:
Widespread,
plutons

LOOKALIKES:
Granodiorite,
diorite

Granite

Chemical group: Acid igneous

Granite and other rocks of the granite family are
the most widely distributed of the deeper
(plutonic) igneous rocks; they are a major
component of the Earth's crust. Alkali feldspar
is the dominant mineral and can form larger
crystals; its colour determines the general colour
of the rock. Granite is hard and tough, widely
used in construction and monuments. Characteristic weathering can lead to rounded topography, relic stacks of granite slabs called 'tors',
as in SW England, and onion-skin exfoliation of
massive boulders, as in South Africa.

FAMILY: GRANITE

ID FACT FILE

ESSENTIAL MINERALS:
Alkali feldspar, plagioclase, quartz

OTHER MINERALS:
Biotite, hornblende, augite, muscovite, apatite, zircon, magnetite

MINERAL PROPORTIONS:
Alkali feldspar> plagioclase> quartz. These 3 minerals make up more than 80% of the rock

COLOUR:
Mottled, grey, pink or yellowish

TEXTURAL FEATURES:
Coarse-grained interlocking crystals; granular, or other textures (*see* main text)

DISTRIBUTION:
Continental crust of all ages

ABUNDANCE:
Widespread, plutons

LOOKALIKES:
Granodiomte diorite

Above:
Graphic granite

Below:
Detail of biotite granite

Granite Varieties

Chemical group: Acid igneous

Graphic granite (illustrated) occurs in pegmatite, and has quartz which resembles Egyptian writing. *Biotite granite* and tourmaline granite have up to 20 per cent of these minerals. *Orbicular granite* is rare; it has orange-sized circular spheres of pale granite within normal granite. *Rapakivi granite* has golf ball-sized spheres of pinkish feldspar surrounded by a matrix of darker granite. *Porphyry* is a granite with two distinct sizes of crystals (porphyritic texture) that tends to occur in small bodies.

FAMILY: GRANITE

ID FACT FILE

ESSENTIAL MINERALS:
Plagioclase,
alkali feldspar,
quartz

OTHER MINERALS:
Biotite,
hornblende,
muscovite,
augite, apatite,
zircon, magnetite

MINERAL PROPORTIONS:
Plagioclase>alkali
feldspar>quartz.
These three
minerals make
up more than
60% of the rock

COLOUR:
Mottled grey,
dark grey

TEXTURAL FEATURES:
Coarse-grained
interlocking
crystals;
granular. Quartz
forms irregular
shapes between
feldspars.
Similar to granite

DISTRIBUTION:
Continental crust
of all ages

ABUNDANCE:
Widespread,
small plutons

LOOKALIKES:
Granite, diorite

Granodiorite

Chemical group: Acid igneous

Granodiorite is similar to granite, except that plagioclase feldspar is more abundant than alkali feldspar, and the rock contains more dark minerals. It is a darker-coloured rock and generally less abundant than granite. Most of the rock is made of feldspars and quartz or 'felsic' minerals. A hand lens should reveal the identity of the mafic minerals, biotite and hornblende; quartz is often vitreous dull grey compared to white or pale grey feldspar. Found in Southern Uplands/Scotland, southern Norway, Germany, Austria.

FAMILY: QUARTZOLITE

ID FACT FILE

ESSENTIAL MINERALS:
Quartz

OTHER MINERALS:
Mica, feldspars, topaz, fluorite, apatite, tourmaline

MINERAL PROPORTIONS:
Quartz>60%

COLOUR:
Pale grey, reddish

TEXTURAL FEATURES:
Coarse-grained interlocking crystals; granular, often with cavities

DISTRIBUTION:
Continental crust

ABUNDANCE:
Restricted to bodies or veins a few hundred metres in size

LOOKALIKES:
Pegmatite

Greisen

Chemical group: Acid igneous

Greisen is a rock made mostly of quartz. It is usually associated with granites and may form when feldspar is removed by hydrothermal fluids long after the granite solidified. Generally light grey or stained brownish by iron. Well-formed and therefore collectable accessory minerals are often found concentrated in patches and cavities, and can include gem material, such as topaz, as in Brazil. Occasionally host to tungsten, tin or molybdenum minerals, as in Cornwall and Devon/England.

FAMILY: FOIDOLITE

Ijolite

Chemical group: Alkaline igneous

Ijolite is mainly composed of just two minerals, nepheline and pyroxene (aegirine-augite or aegirine). Nepheline forms square-shaped crystals set amongst black pyroxene. It occurs as small bodies in association with alkaline igneous rocks like nepheline syenite, and with alkaline volcanic rocks like phonolite, nephelinite and carbonatite. Relatively young ijolites are found in the East African Rift Valley. Older ijolites are found in Norway, Sweden, Finland, Kola/Russia and Brazil. The photograph shows a variety with very large pyroxene.

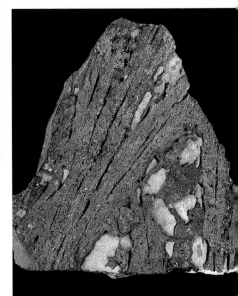

Kimberlite

Chemical group: Alkaline igneous

ID FACT FILE

ESSENTIAL MINERALS:
Olivine,
pyroxene,
phlogopite

OTHER MINERALS:
Pyrope, ilmenite,
chromite (spinel),
calcite,
serpentine,
perovskite

MINERAL PROPORTIONS:
Olivine>pyroxene
>phlogopite

COLOUR:
Greenish to
bluish

TEXTURAL FEATURES:
Large, often
rounded crystals
of olivine

DISTRIBUTION:
Occurs in areas
of old or ancient
continental crust

ABUNDANCE:
Uncommon

LOOKALIKES:
Picrite

Kimberlite is an olivine-rich rock, with a distinctive porphyritic texture (having minerals of two sizes). The olivine is often altered to serpentine. It is often characterised by its minor minerals, which include red pyrope, brown phlogopite and apple-green diopside. It is also famous for hosting diamonds. It forms vertical pipe-like bodies with ice cream cone-shaped tops called diatremes, and also dykes and sills. Found in Kimberley/South Africa, Zaire, Tanzania, India, Siberia/Russia, Brazil, Canada. The photograph is of octahedral diamond in kimberlite.

FAMILY: LAMPROPHYRE

ID FACT FILE

ESSENTIAL MINERALS:
Augite, mica, hornblende, plagioclase, orthoclase

OTHER MINERALS:
Olivine or quartz, magnetite, apatite

MINERAL PROPORTIONS:
Mostly dark minerals

COLOUR:
Dark-coloured

TEXTURAL FEATURES:
Larger dark-coloured crystals (phenocrysts) set in finely crystalline or glassy matrix of feldspar

DISTRIBUTION:
Peripheral to large plutons or subvolcanic

ABUNDANCE:
Common

LOOKALIKES:
Basalt, dolerite

Lamprophyre

Chemical group: Intermediate igneous

Lamprophyre is a general name for fine-grained dark igneous rock with two sizes of crystals (porphyritic texture) but no large crystals of feldspar; compare with andesite (*see* p.161), which is the opposite. Its dark colour reflects the high proportions of dark minerals, which can vary greatly. It usually forms small bodies, such as dykes, sometimes at the edge of larger intrusions. *Minette* is a mica-rich variety related to syenite. Found in Southern Uplands/Scotland, Devon/England, Oberpfalz/Bavaria/Germany, Vosges/France.

FAMILY: SYENITE

ID FACT FILE

ESSENTIAL MINERALS:
Alkali feldspar, plagioclase, augite, biotite

OTHER MINERALS:
Hornblende, magnetite, apatite, zircon, titanite, nepheline or quartz

MINERAL PROPORTIONS:
Alkali feldspar dominant

COLOUR:
Dark grey, greenish, bluish. Distinctive internal peacock colours in large feldspar crystals

TEXTURAL FEATURES:
Coarse-grained rock with larger crystals of feldspar, and small clots of dark minerals

DISTRIBUTION:
Related to alkaline volcanism and continental rifting

ABUNDANCE:
Restricted

LOOKALIKES:
Unlikely to be mistaken

Larvikite

Chemical group: Alkaline igneous

Larvikite is a well-known variety of syenite, valued for decorative purposes; polishing enhances the play of peacock colours in the feldspar (a variety of alkali feldspar but similar in appearance to labradorite; *see* plagioclase, p.93). The texture shows large feldspar crystals and small clots of dark minerals, which include biotite and other minerals. Larvikite occurs in large igneous plutonic bodies related to an old (Permian age) volcanic rift around Larvik near Oslo, Norway. It is from this site that the rock takes its name.

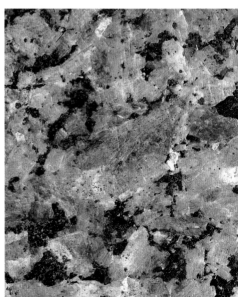

ID FACT FILE

ESSENTIAL MINERALS:
Plagioclase,
hypersthene,
augite

OTHER MINERALS:
Olivine,
hornblende,
spinel, ilmenite,
magnetite,
apatite

MINERAL PROPORTIONS:
Plagioclase>
pyroxene

COLOUR:
Dark grey,
greenish,
brownish

TEXTURAL FEATURES:
Granitic texture,
crystals
intergrown; may
show alignment
of platy
feldspars, or
layering

DISTRIBUTION:
Deeper
continental crust;
uplifted oceanic
crust

ABUNDANCE:
Common

LOOKALIKES:
Gabbro

Norite

Chemical group: Basic igneous

Norite is a variety of gabbro (*see* p.183), characterised by the dominance of hypersthene as the dark-coloured mineral in the rock. Often difficult to distinguish, unless the bronzy lustre of cleaved surfaces of hypersthene is visible. The famous nickel sulphide deposit at Sudbury/Canada is associated with a large body of norite.

ID FACT FILE

ESSENTIAL MINERALS:
Alkali feldspar
and either quartz
or feldspathoid

OTHER MINERALS:
Variable e g
albite,
tourmaline,
topaz, beryl,
mica, apatite,
zircon, titanite
and rare
minerals

MINERAL PROPORTIONS:
Distinctive
texture

COLOUR:
Pale-coloured

TEXTURAL FEATURES:
Very large
crystals, often
perfectly formed;
giant crystals are
known

DISTRIBUTION:
Occurs in small
bodies within or
adjacent to large
igneous masses
of granites and
syenites

ABUNDANCE:
Widespread

LOOKALIKES:
None

Pegmatite

Chemical group: Acid or alkaline igneous

Pegmatite is purely a textural term for the
coarsest grain size of igneous rocks. Distinctive
large crystals (cm-scale) are often perfectly
formed, sometimes protruding into voids. The
alkali feldspar can be orthoclase, or microcline
and albite (plagioclase) may also occur.
Pegmatites are the main source of many gem
minerals, such as pink and green tourmaline
and spodumene found in granite pegmatites
from California/USA and Brazil, and
aquamarine and emerald from Colombia; in
addition, tin, copper, tungsten and other metal
mineralisation is often associated with granite
pegmatites, as in Cornwall/England. Pegmatites
associated with nepheline syenites often contain
nepheline, zircon, titanite and rare earth
element minerals, as around Oslo/Norway.

ID FACT FILE

ESSENTIAL MINERALS:
Alkali feldspar,
plagioclase,
nepheline or
quartz

OTHER MINERALS:
Pyroxene, biotite,
amphibole,
magnetite,
apatite, zircon,
titanite

**MINERAL
PROPORTIONS:**
Alkali feldspar>
plagioclase>less
mafic minerals

COLOUR:
Light to dark
grey, reddish,
brownish

TEXTURAL FEATURES:
Medium- to
coarse-grained
rock with larger
crystals of
feldspar and
small clots of
dark minerals

DISTRIBUTION:
Related to old
alkaline
volcanism and
continental rifting

ABUNDANCE:
Restricted

LOOKALIKES:
Granite has
much more
quartz

Syenite

Chemical group: Alkaline igneous

Syenite is a feldspar-rich coarse-grained rock
that is similar in many respects to granite, but
has little or no quartz; instead of quartz it
often contains the feldspathoid nepheline. The
pyroxene is alkali-rich aegirine or aegirine-
augite. Found at Borrolan/Scotland,
Saxony/Germany, Oslo/Norway, southern
Portugal, Kola/Russia, Piemonte/Italy,
Transvaal/South Africa.

There are several varieties of syenite.
Nepheline syenite (*foyaite*) contains substantial
nepheline and often has tabular feldspars, as in
southern Portugal; it may also contain sodalite.
Monzonite contains about equal proportions of
orthoclase and plagioclase, as in S Tyrol/Italy.
Larvikite is another variety (*see* p.191).

Syenite Varieties
Chemical group: Alkaline igneous

Nepheline syenite (foyaite)

Monzonite

FAMILY: GRANITE

ID FACT FILE

ESSENTIAL MINERALS:
Plagioclase, quartz, biotite, hornblende

OTHER MINERALS:
Alkali feldspar, muscovite, augite, apatite, zircon, magnetite

MINERAL PROPORTIONS:
Plagioclase> alkali feldspar> quartz. These three minerals make up more than 60% of the rock

COLOUR:
Dark grey, mottled

TEXTURAL FEATURES:
Coarse-grained interlocking crystals; granular. Similar to granite. Dark minerals may be slightly larger

DISTRIBUTION:
Continental crust of all ages

ABUNDANCE:
Common, small plutons

LOOKALIKES:
Granite, granodiorite

Tonalite

Chemical group: Intermediate igneous

Tonalite is a variety of granodiorite with almost no alkali feldspar. The colour reflects the colour of plagioclase (grey) and is darker. Hornblende and biotite can occur as larger crystals in a pale matrix, giving a characteristic spotted appearance, as in Tonale district/S Tyrol/Italy, southern Norway, Finland, Sweden. The variety *trondhjemite* is similar to tonalite but has higher quartz content and less dark minerals (<15 per cent).

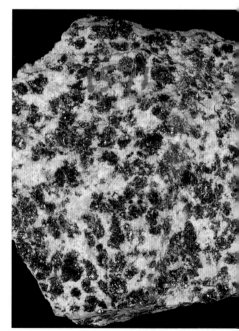

FAMILY: GABBRO

Troctolite

Chemical group: Basic igneous

ID FACT FILE

ESSENTIAL MINERALS:
Plagioclase, olivine

OTHER MINERALS:
Pyroxenes, spinel, magnetite, apatite

MINERAL PROPORTIONS:
Plagioclase> olivine

COLOUR:
Dark grey, greenish, brownish

TEXTURAL FEATURES:
Granitic texture, crystals intergrown with clots of dark minerals

DISTRIBUTION:
Continental crust

ABUNDANCE:
Common

LOOKALIKES:
Gabbro, anorthosite

Troctolite, also known as trout stone, is a variety of gabbro (*see* p.183). It is characterised by its generally pale colour and its spotted appearance, which is formed by clots of dark minerals; olivine is the chief mafic mineral. Where fresh, olivine in the rock is green, but where altered, olivine is frequently replaced by serpentine minerals, giving the rock a reddish or brownish colour. It occurs with other gabbros in larger intrusive complexes as at Ardnamurchan/Scotland.

FAMILY: AMPHIBOLITE

ID FACT FILE

TYPICAL MINERALS:
Hornblende,
plagioclase

OTHER MINERALS:
Quartz, biotite,
chlorite, garnet,
epidote, zoisite

MINERAL PROPORTIONS:
Abundant
amphibole

GRAIN SIZE:
Fine to coarse-
grained, even-
textured;
massive or
schist-like

COLOUR:
Dark grey,
greenish, black

TEXTURAL FEATURES:
Even-textured
rock, elongated
amphibole
crystals
sometimes
aligned

FOLIATION:
Usually poor;
occasionally
distinctive and
schist-like

CONDITIONS:
Low–moderate
pressure,
moderate–high
temperature

DISTRIBUTION:
Widespread

LOOKALIKES:
Basalt/gabbro

Amphibolite

Chemical group: Basic/intermediate

Amphibolite is a typical medium-grade regional metamorphic rock. In addition to hornblende and sodium-calcium-rich plagioclase, it frequently contains quartz or garnet, as in *garnet amphibolite*. Amphibolite is the hydrous product of metamorphism of basic igneous rocks like gabbro and dolerite. It can form massive bodies, and also retain recognisable basalt-like intrusive forms such as dykes. Found in Grampian Mountains and NW Scotland, Donegal and Connemara/Ireland, Hohe Tauern/Austria, St Gotthard/Switzerland, Baden and Bavaria/Germany, Scandinavia.

ID FACT FILE

TYPICAL MINERALS:
Essential blue amphibole (glaucophane)

OTHER MINERALS:
Epidote, albite, calcite, garnet, quartz, zoisite, jadeite, mica, talc

MINERAL PROPORTIONS:
Plentiful glaucophane, others variable

GRAIN SIZE:
Fine- to medium-grained

COLOUR:
Dark bluish grey

TEXTURAL FEATURES:
Parallel fabric of glaucophane forms planes of weakness; rock cleaves into thin platy pieces

FOLIATION:
Strong, parallel to platy minerals; often wavy

CONDITIONS:
High pressure, low temperature

DISTRIBUTION:
Rare but characteristic of old subducted oceanic crust; ophiolites

LOOKALIKES:
Unlikely to be mistaken

Blueschist

Chemical group: Basic/intermediate

Blueschist is the highest pressure variety of schist that forms at rather low temperatures from old subducted oceanic crust. The bluish colour is quite distinctive, often associated with minor yellowish-green epidote and minor garnet. Found at southern Brittany/France, Anglesey/Wales, Tuscany/Italy, Spitzbergen, Channel Islands, Western Alps, California/USA, Cyprus.

ID FACT FILE

TYPICAL MINERALS:
Pyroxene, garnet

OTHER MINERALS:
Amphibole, kyanite, rutile, zoisite, plagioclase, quartz

MINERAL PROPORTIONS:
Garnet and pyroxene in similar amounts

GRAIN SIZE:
Medium, coarse

COLOUR:
Grey, greenish, reddish

TEXTURAL FEATURES:
Prominent rounded garnets in a matrix of pyroxene crystals

FOLIATION:
Weak to moderate; often massive unfoliated

CONDITIONS:
Very high pressure, high temperature

DISTRIBUTION:
Rare, small bodies in high-grade terrains

LOOKALIKES:
Garnet amphibolite

Eclogite

Chemical group: Basic/ultrabasic

Eclogite is a dark-coloured granular rock with distinctive reddish or orangy garnet (pyrope, almandine) set in a matrix of greenish pyroxene (omphacite). Other minerals are present in only minor amounts. It forms by high-grade metamorphism of basic igneous rocks like basalt, and is one of the products of subducted oceanic crust. It has the highest density (3.2–3.6) of silicate rocks in the crust. It occurs at Glenelg/Scotland, Hohe Tauern/Austria, Schwarzwald and Fichtelberg/Germany, California/USA. It also occurs as xenoliths in kimberlite (*see* p.189) transported from the mantle. It is distinguished from amphibolite by its paler colour.

ID FACT FILE

TYPICAL MINERALS:
Alkali feldspar, plagioclase, quartz, biotite

OTHER MINERALS:
Hornblende, garnet, cordierite, muscovite, sillimanite

MINERAL PROPORTIONS:
Alkali feldspar always present

GRAIN SIZE:
Coarse; variable across outcrop

COLOUR:
Often banded dark and light; grey, reddish, brownish, greenish

TEXTURAL FEATURES:
Prominent, discontinuous banding due to repeated variation in proportions of dark and light minerals

FOLIATION:
Weak to distinct, parallel to dark mica-rich bands

CONDITIONS:
High pressure, moderate–high temperature

DISTRIBUTION:
Widespread

LOOKALIKES:
Migmatite, schist

Gneiss

Chemical group: Intermediate/acid

Gneiss is perhaps the commonest regional metamorphic rock type. It is coarse-grained and often granite-like in composition, with abundant feldspars and quartz separated by bands of dark minerals, usually rich in biotite. Strong preferred orientation of the biotite leads to a preferred breaking direction, or foliation. Varieties are named according to characteristic mineral (garnet-gneiss, cordierite-gneiss, etc) or textural features, and include *augen gneiss*, which has distinctive eye-shaped large alkali feldspar crystals. Occurs at NW Scotland, Central Alps, Massif Central and Brittany/France, Norway, Sweden, Finland, Bayerischer Wald/Germany, Canadian Shield.

FAMILY: GRANULITE

ID FACT FILE

TYPICAL MINERALS:
Alkali feldspar, plagioclase, quartz

OTHER MINERALS:
Pyroxene, garnet, cordierite, sillimanite, kyanite, scapolite

MINERAL PROPORTIONS:
Gneiss-like but no mica; variable

GRAIN SIZE:
Medium- to fine-grained

COLOUR:
Grey, brownish, greenish

TEXTURAL FEATURES:
Even-textured, sugary grain size; often finely banded

FOLIATION:
Weak; sometimes absent

CONDITIONS:
High pressure and high temperature

DISTRIBUTION:
Widespread, typical rock of lowermost crust

LOOKALIKES:
Hornfels does not occur over large regional distances

Granulite

Chemical group: Intermediate/acid

Granulite is an even-textured high-grade metamorphic rock with weak or absent foliation. Often fine parallel bands of dark minerals run through the rock. Garnet-granulite and pyroxene-granulite are thought to be typical rocks from the lowermost continental crust. *Charnockite* is a variety with igneous interlocking texture, without garnet, but often containing hypersthene. Granulites occur in NW Scotland, Austria, Czechoslovakia, Finland, Saxony/Germany, India. Also as xenoliths in some continental volcanoes.

FAMILY: SCHIST

Greenschist

Chemical group: Basic/intermediate

ID FACT FILE

TYPICAL MINERALS:
Chlorite, epidote, actinolite, albite

OTHER MINERALS:
Glaucophane, talc, calcite, magnetite, dolomite, quartz

MINERAL PROPORTIONS:
Abundant green minerals; quartz and orthoclase very minor or absent

GRAIN SIZE:
Fine-grained

COLOUR:
Dark or light greenish grey

TEXTURAL FEATURES:
Even-textured rock, prominent platy weakness due to alignment of platy minerals (schist)

FOLIATION:
Distinct like schist

CONDITIONS:
Low–moderate pressure, moderate temperature

DISTRIBUTION:
Widespread; typical product of metamorphosed basic igneous rocks

LOOKALIKES:
Schist

The main minerals in greenschist contain large amounts of iron, magnesium and calcium, plus the feldspar albite. The dominant greenish-coloured mineral is usually chlorite, but many varieties of greenschist are dominated by different green minerals, such as *actinolite schist*, *chlorite schist*, and *talc schist*. Found at Argyle/Scotland, Hohe Tauern/Tyrol/Austria, Harz, Fichtelgebirge and Bavaria/Germany, S Tyrol and Piemonte/Italy, Western Alps.

ID FACT FILE

TYPICAL MINERALS:
Andalusite,
biotite,
cordierite,
garnet,
hypersthene,
sillimanite,
quartz, feldspar

OTHER MINERALS:
Variable

MINERAL PROPORTIONS:
Variable;
substantial
feldspar

GRAIN SIZE:
Fine- to medium-
grained

COLOUR:
Dark-coloured,
grey, greenish,
black

TEXTURAL FEATURES:
Even-textured
rock, often
granular

FOLIATION:
None

CONDITIONS:
Low–moderate
pressure, high
temperature

DISTRIBUTION:
Contact
metamorphic
rock developed
adjacent to large
igneous
intrusions

LOOKALIKES:
Basalt,
amphibolite

Hornfels

Chemical group: Any

Hornfels is the general name for hard rock developed in contact with large igneous intrusions. Hornfels often has a conchoidal fracture and is very tough and weather-resistant. Although it often contains many pale-coloured minerals, the rock colour is usually dark due to the very fine grain size. There are many varieties, the names of which are based on the dominant minerals, e g *andalusite hornfels* and *pyroxene hornfels*; other varieties are named after the precursor rock, as in *pelitic hornfels*. Found in Dartmoor, Cornwall and Cumbria/England, Southern Uplands/Scotland, Vosges/France, Harz and Eifel/Germany, southern Norway. Below: photomicrograph under crossed polars, greatly magnified

Lherzolite

Chemical group: Ultrabasic

Lherzolite is the most typical variety of olivine-rich rocks called peridotites; it contains mostly olivine, and smaller but similar amounts of enstatite and diopside. It is thought to be the dominant rock in the Earth's upper mantle. Its granular texture is developed under conditions of high pressure over long periods of time. Dark red garnet (pyrope) and small black grains of chromite are often present. During repeated metamorphism at lower pressure in the presence of water, the olivine in peridotite is replaced by serpentine and talc, sometimes producing serpentine rock (serpentinite; *see* p.212). Found at Lherz/Pyrenees, Central Alps, Cyprus, Ronda/Spain. Also found as xenoliths in kimberlite and some volcanoes.

FAMILY: MARBLE

ID FACT FILE

TYPICAL MINERALS:
Calcite, dolomite

OTHER MINERALS:
Amphibole, forsterite, epidote, mica, garnet, magnetite, plagioclase, pyrite, quartz, serpentine, wollastonite

MINERAL PROPORTIONS:
Mostly carbonate

GRAIN SIZE:
Coarse-grained; massive

COLOUR:
White, pale pinkish, greenish, grey; variegated or banded

TEXTURAL FEATURES:
Compact, often wavy or stripy appearance

FOLIATION:
None to well-foliated

CONDITIONS:
Low–moderate pressure, moderate–high temperature

DISTRIBUTION:
Widespread in mountain belts, also around igneous intrusions

LOOKALIKES:
Limestone

Marble

Chemical group: Carbonate-rich

Marble is a coarsely crystalline calcite-rich metamorphic rock. It develops smooth, sometimes grooved, weathered surfaces and is sparkling or granular in broken surfaces. It is pale-coloured and translucent. Its even strength makes it a popular stone for building and ornamental purposes, although it is rather soft since it is made mostly of calcite. It is the typical product of metamorphosed limestone; a wide variety of minor minerals is often present. It can be distinguished from limestone by its lack of cavities, lack of fossils and coarse grain texture of shiny calcite grains ('sparry' texture). Found at Devon/England, Connemara/Ireland, Skye/Scotland, Tuscany and S Tyrol/Italy, Tyrol/Austria, France, Fichtelgebirge/Germany, Spain and Greece.

FAMILY: MARBLE

Marble Variety

Migmatite

Chemical group: Intermediate/acid

ID FACT FILE

TYPICAL MINERALS:
Alkali feldspar, plagioclase, quartz, biotite

OTHER MINERALS:
Hornblende, garnet, cordierite, muscovite, sillimanite

MINERAL PROPORTIONS:
Alkali feldspar always present; quartz-rich segregations

GRAIN SIZE:
Coarse; variable across outcrop

COLOUR:
Often banded with white segregations

TEXTURAL FEATURES:
Prominent gneiss-like banding and interfingering of whitish segregations and snake-like folds

FOLIATION:
Weak to distinct, parallel to dark mica-rich bands

CONDITIONS:
Low–high pressure, very high temperature

DISTRIBUTION:
Widespread

LOOKALIKES:
Gneiss

Migmatite appears as two intermingled rocks; usually the host gneiss is permeated by decimetre- to metre-scale white or light-coloured granite-like rock. Migmatite represents one of the highest grades of regional metamorphism; the granite portion indicates a nearly-melted or partially melted condition (also called *anatexis*). Occurs at NW Scotland, Central Alps, Brittany and Auvergne/France, Norway, Sweden, Finland, Black Forest and Bavaria/Germany, Adirondacks and Washington/USA.

FAMILY: SCHIST

ID FACT FILE

TYPICAL MINERALS:
Mica, quartz

OTHER MINERALS:
Biotite, feldspar, chlorite, pyrophyllite, graphite, epidote

MINERAL PROPORTIONS:
Abundant mica (sericite)

GRAIN SIZE:
Fine-grained; speckled with occasional larger crystals

COLOUR:
Pale silvery grey, pale greenish

TEXTURAL FEATURES:
Even-textured rock, flaky sericite wraps around other granular crystals; strong alignment and fine-scale wavy fabric

FOLIATION:
Prominent distinctive schist; cleaves into thin sheets

CONDITIONS:
Low–moderate pressure, moderate–high temperature

DISTRIBUTION:
Widespread

LOOKALIKES:
Other schists

Phyllite

Chemical group: Intermediate

Phyllite is a pale-coloured schist that is rich in the mica sericite, and can be split readily into thin sheets; it has a distinctive silky lustre on fresh surfaces. Contains a number of other flaky minerals whose parallel alignment can produce sheet-like foliation. The presence of abundant quartz can be tested with hardness (scratches knife), but most other minerals are too small to identify even with a hand lens. Found Cornwall/England, Vosges/France, Harz/Germany, Central Alps, Scandinavia, NW Highlands/Scotland. Below: enlargement with a hand lens.

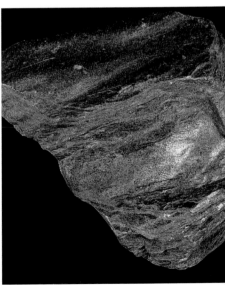

FAMILY: QUARTZITE

ID FACT FILE

TYPICAL MINERALS:
Quartz

OTHER MINERALS:
Any rock-forming minerals, e g feldspar, mica, chlorite, garnet

MINERAL PROPORTIONS:
Abundant quartz (>80%)

GRAIN SIZE:
Fine- to coarse-grained; massive

COLOUR:
White, grey, brownish, reddish

TEXTURAL FEATURES:
Even-textured, massive

FOLIATION:
Absent or inconspicuous

CONDITIONS:
Low–moderate pressure, low–moderate temperature

DISTRIBUTION:
Widespread; typical product of metamorphosed sedimentary sandstone, quartz arenite

LOOKALIKES:
Sedimentary quartzite, sandstone

Quartzite

Chemical group: Acid

Quartzite forms thick layers in metamorphic mountain belts that are resistant to weathering. Original sedimentary quartz grains are strongly cemented by further interlocking quartz, producing a tough, often feature-forming rock. Minor amounts of iron-rich minerals cause reddening. Some varieties contain reasonable amounts of mica, enabling the rock to split into regular slabs. Irregular quartz grains are visible with a hand lens (*see* view below). Occurs at Anglesey/Wales, Highlands/Scotland, Harz/Germany, Steiermark/Austria, Scandinavia, Pyrenees/Spain.

Schist

Chemical group: Basic/intermediate

ID FACT FILE

TYPICAL MINERALS:
Essential platy minerals like mica, chlorite, amphibole or talc

OTHER MINERALS:
Quartz, feldspar, epidote, graphite, garnet, cordierite, sillimanite, calcite, magnetite

MINERAL PROPORTIONS:
Variable

GRAIN SIZE:
Fine-grained, sometimes with coarser crystals

COLOUR:
Often pale grey, greenish; distinctive sheen from reflective minerals

TEXTURAL FEATURES:
Parallel fabric of platy minerals; rock cleaves into platy pieces

FOLIATION:
Strong, often wavy

CONDITIONS:
Moderate–high pressure and temperature

DISTRIBUTION:
Widespread, large regions of old continental crust

LOOKALIKES:
Amphibolite, gneiss

Schist is a widely distributed metamorphic rock, recognised by its strong foliation and ease of parting. It is a textural rock name and wide mineral variations lead to many named varieties of schist. *Mica schist* with abundant muscovite, biotite or chlorite is the usual and best recognised variety, displaying shiny surfaces when broken. Dark red or brownish garnet in pale grey *garnet-mica schist* often weathers to rusty brown spots. Other varieties of schist are described separately. Occurs in Scotland, Connemara/Ireland, Central Alps, Scandinavia, Germany, Central Pyrenees, France, Spain.

FAMILY: SERPENTINITE

ID FACT FILE

TYPICAL MINERALS:
Serpentine

OTHER MINERALS:
Talc, calcite,
olivine, pyroxene,
amphibole,
magnetite,
garnet, chromite

MINERAL PROPORTIONS:
Abundant
serpentine
(chrysotile,
antigorite)

GRAIN SIZE:
Fine- to coarse-
grained

COLOUR:
Dark green,
greenish grey,
dark red to black

TEXTURAL FEATURES:
Massive or
fibrous;
sometimes
schist-like

FOLIATION:
Usually absent,
but sometimes
distinctive like
schist

CONDITIONS:
Low–high
pressure, low
temperature

DISTRIBUTION:
Restricted
product of
metamorphosed
ultramafic rocks

LOOKALIKES:
Peridotite

Serpentinite

Chemical group: Ultrabasic/basic

Serpentinite is a metamorphosed ultramafic
rock where both olivine and pyroxene have
been converted to serpentine minerals.
Smaller amounts of a wide variety of minerals
often include calcite and talc. A soft rock, it
weathers to rounded shapes, is easily carved
with a knife and occurs in a wide variety of
colours. Sometimes used for ornamental or
decorative purposes, as at Lizard/Cornwall/
England. Also found at Shetland Isles/
Scotland, Austria, Pyrenees, Switzerland,
Liguria/Italy, Vosges/France, Fichtelgebirge/
Germany, Troödos/Cyprus.

ID FACT FILE

TYPICAL MINERALS:
Calcite, wollastonite, diopside, tremolite

OTHER MINERALS:
Dolomite, garnet, vesuvianite, serpentine, quartz

MINERAL PROPORTIONS:
Variable, often zoned

GRAIN SIZE:
Fine- to coarse-grained

COLOUR:
Pale grey, greenish, brownish

TEXTURAL FEATURES:
Granular, sometimes banded

FOLIATION:
None

CONDITIONS:
Low–moderate pressure, high temperature

DISTRIBUTION:
Restricted to contact metamorphosed limestone around igneous intrusions

LOOKALIKES:
Marble

Skarn

Chemical group: Calcium-carbonate-silicate

Skarns are produced by contact metamorphism of limestones. They change progressively from rather pure carbonate marble to bands made of various calcium-magnesium silicate minerals, and finally to a carbonate-free silicate rock. They are zoned towards the igneous heat source. A common pattern grades from unaltered dolomite to a tremolite zone, then to a narrower diopside zone and finally to an inner wollastonite and garnet zone. Found at Skye/Scotland, Dartmoor/England, Elba/Italy, Bavaria/Germany, Sweden.

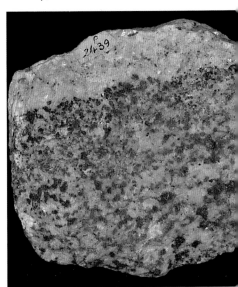

Slate

Chemical group: Intermediate/acid

Slate results from low-grade regional metamorphism of fine-grained sedimentary mudrocks. The most obvious feature is the presence of parallel planes of weakness, along which the rock splits easily (cleavage), making it distinct from original sedimentary bedding. Fossils can be preserved, though they may be deformed and partly replaced by pyrite. When further heated during contact with a large igneous intrusion, additional minerals, such as andalusite, can give the slate a spotted appearance. Widely used as a roofing material. Found at Cumbria and Devon/England, Wales, Ardennes/France, Fichtelgebirge and Saxony/Germany.

ID FACT FILE

Typical minerals:
Mica, chlorite, quartz, feldspar

Other minerals:
Graphite, pyrite

Mineral proportions:
Abundant mica and chlorite

Grain size:
Very fine-grained

Colour:
Dark grey, greenish, bluish grey

Textural features:
Even-textured rock with pronounced uniform cleavage direction

Foliation:
Distinctive slaty cleavage, can be split into thin flakes

Conditions:
Low pressure, low temperature

Distribution:
Widespread; typical product of metamorphosed sedimentary mudrocks

Lookalikes:
Unlikely to be mistaken

ID FACT FILE

TYPICAL COMPONENTS:
Quartz, feldspar, lithic fragments

OTHER COMPONENTS:
Haematite, calcite, clay, mica, resistant minerals

MATERIAL PROPORTIONS:
Feldspar>25%; much quartz and lithic fragments

GRAIN SIZE:
$\frac{1}{16}$ to 2 mm

COLOUR:
Reddish brown, dark red

TEXTURAL FEATURES:
Continuous layering due to bedding planes; sedimentary structures and indications of mechanical sorting of grains

DISTRIBUTION:
Widespread surface-formed regional rock type known from all different geological ages

LOOKALIKES:
Sandstone

Arkose

Chemical group: Acid

Arkose is a sedimentary rock with a high feldspar content (usually orthoclase or microcline), derived from weathering of feldspar-rich rocks like granites and gneisses. It contains some rock fragments and micas in a fine-grained matrix. The presence of haematite and iron staining cause the red coloration. Outcrop-scale features show evidence of sedimentation including, usually, bedding planes, sedimentary structures and sorting of grains by layers. Occurs in Precambrian 'Torridonian sandstone' in part and Devonian-aged rocks, 'Old Red Sandstone' in part, as at Torridon in NW Scotland, Devon/England and Vosges/France.

FAMILY: COARSE CLASTIC SEDIMENT

ID FACT FILE

TYPICAL COMPONENTS:
Lithic fragments, quartz and feldspar

OTHER COMPONENTS:
Haematite, calcite, clay, mica, resistant minerals

MATERIAL PROPORTIONS:
Variable

GRAIN SIZE:
Dominant mixture of granules (2–4 mm) and pebbles (4–64 mm), locally with cobbles (64–256 mm) or even boulders (>256 mm)

COLOUR:
Often brightly coloured, yellow, reddish, grey

TEXTURAL FEATURES:
Unsorted mixture of grain sizes and angular clasts; originally porous then cemented by quartz, calcite or clay minerals

DISTRIBUTION:
Restricted to continental areas with high relief, eg mountains

LOOKALIKES:
Conglomerate has rounded clasts and may be bedded

Breccia

Chemical group: Intermediate/acid

Breccia is a distinctive rock due to the presence of abundant angular and irregular-shaped rock fragments of varying sizes. The rock fragments vary widely depending on the source area. There is usually no sedimentary bedding and fossils are absent from the matrix. Slump breccias form by hillwash or landslide deposits; solution breccias result from cavity collapse and dissolution of evaporites beneath overlying rocks. Found at Mendips/England, Western Alps, Pyrenees/France and Spain, and S Tyrol and Sicily/Italy. *Tillite* is a hardened variety with boulders supported in a fine sand or clay matrix deposited under ice by ancient glaciations.

FAMILY: SILICEOUS SEDIMENT

ID FACT FILE

TYPICAL COMPONENTS:
Silica

OTHER COMPONENTS:
Minor clay, haematite

MATERIAL PROPORTIONS:
Mostly silica

GRAIN SIZE:
Very fine-grained, no visible crystals

COLOUR:
Black, grey, greenish or reddish

TEXTURAL FEATURES:
Very hard and compact, brittle fracture; occurs in bedded or nodular layers

DISTRIBUTION:
Moderate to deep water; bedded cherts may be associated with volcanic rocks. Widely distributed in rocks of all ages

LOOKALIKES:
Flint is a variety

Chert

Chemical group: Acid

Chert is composed almost entirely of very fine-grained silica, and includes some forms of opal and chalcedony. Its very fine grain size gives it a dark colour. There are two types of chert. Bedded cherts can be extensive regional rock units, and may be related to hydrothermal activity or enhanced biochemical activity associated with volcanism. Nodular chert usually occurs in carbonate rocks as large irregular rounded lumps; small lumps in chalk are called *flint*. Biogenic silica, originally dispersed throughout the rock, for example as sponge spicules, is reprecipitated by fluids into the concentrations we see as chert. Found at Dover and Yorkshire/England, Ballantrae/Scotland, Montagne Noire/France, Mittelharz and Bavaria/Germany, Pyrenees/Spain and France, Cyprus.

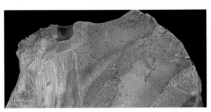

above chert   *below* flint

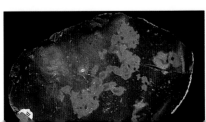

FAMILY: CLASTIC SEDIMENT

ID FACT FILE

TYPICAL COMPONENTS:
Clay minerals

OTHER COMPONENTS:
Quartz, feldspar, micas, calcite, rock dust

MATERIAL PROPORTIONS:
Rich in clay minerals

GRAIN SIZE:
Clay-sized muds (<$\frac{1}{256}$ mm) are finer than silts (<$\frac{1}{16}$ mm)

COLOUR:
Grey, bluish, reddish, brownish, yellowish; variegated

TEXTURAL FEATURES:
Finely laminated, massive; deforms plastically when wet

DISTRIBUTION:
Old river systems, alluvial plains, lake basins

LOOKALIKES:
When dry resemble mudstones

Clay

Chemical group: Intermediate/acid

Clays and claystones contain abundant hydrous clay minerals, largely derived from weathering of feldspars in continental crustal rocks. Clay minerals require X-ray identification, and include kaolinite (*see* p.142), illite and montmorillonite. Their variable colours are caused by additional minerals; limonite gives yellows, haematite browns and reds, sulphides grey, blue and black. Water is trapped in clay, but clay itself is impermeable to water flow and is often used as a barrier. *Bentonite* is a grey-white variety often derived from weathering of volcanic ash. *Boulder clay* is a mixture of boulders in a rock flour and clay matrix formed by icy glaciers. Found in most countries, such as Jurassic age Kimmeridge Clay at Yorkshire/England, central and southern England.

FAMILY: ORGANIC/CARBONACEOUS SEDIMENT

ID FACT FILE

TYPICAL COMPONENTS:
Carbon, organic matter, fossils

OTHER COMPONENTS:
Minor clay, pyrite, quartz, calcite, dolomite, tar

MATERIAL PROPORTIONS:
Various organic compounds of carbon and hydrocarbons

GRAIN SIZE:
Very fine-grained, no visible crystals

COLOUR:
Black, brown

TEXTURAL FEATURES:
Occurs in bedded or slightly nodular layers often with shales and sandstones in repetitive sequences

DISTRIBUTION:
Shallow water, estuaries, swamps; older higher grade coals occur in folded mountain belts

LOOKALIKES:
Unlikely to be mistaken (black streak)

Coal

Chemical group: Organic

Coals are formed from the accumulation and maturation of plant materials. *Peat*, as currently found in moors and fens, is related to coals but is uncompacted and immature. *Anthracite* is the most carbon-rich mature form of coal, the highest grade with more than 90 per cent carbon. It is a bright shiny rock with conchoidal fracture. During maturation of coals, large quantities of hydrocarbon gases, like methane, are released. High-grade coals are generally older, such as those that developed in the Carboniferous age of western Europe. Found at Durham, Northumberland and Yorkshire/ England, S Wales, Midland Valley/Scotland, Essen and Ruhr/Germany.

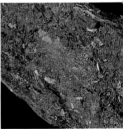
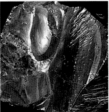

above left coal
above peat
left anthracite coal

ID FACT FILE

TYPICAL COMPONENTS:
Lithic fragments, quartz, feldspar

OTHER COMPONENTS:
Haematite, calcite, clay, mica, resistant minerals

MATERIAL PROPORTIONS:
Variable

GRAIN SIZE:
Dominant mixture of granules (2–4 mm) and pebbles (4–64 mm), locally with cobbles (64–256 mm) or even boulders (>256 mm)

COLOUR:
Often brightly coloured, yellow, reddish, grey

TEXTURAL FEATURES:
Poorly sorted mixture of grain sizes and rounded clasts; cemented by quartz, calcite or clay minerals. May show some bedding or poor grading

DISTRIBUTION:
Sedimentary basins

LOOKALIKES:
Breccia has angular clasts and is unsorted

Conglomerate
Chemical group: Acid

Conglomerate is a coarse clastic rock with distinctive rounded pebbles and other sized clasts of older rocks. Polymict conglomerates show a wide variety of rock types, whereas monomict conglomerates consist of one rock type only eg limestone conglomerate. Conglomerates accumulate within sedimentary basins and alluvial fans or old gravel deposits; they may be clast-supported or matrix-supported. Found at Devon/England, Torridon/Scotland, Upper Bavaria/Germany, Wallis/Switzerland, Sicily/Italy, Pyrenees/France and Spain. Hertfordshire *Puddingstone* (illustrated) is a colourful quartz-cemented variety of Eocene age (45 million years) from central England.

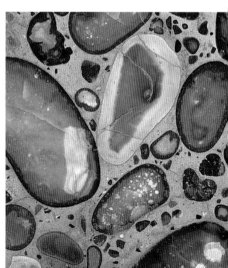

FAMILY: CARBONATE SEDIMENT

ID FACT FILE

TYPICAL COMPONENTS:
Dolomite, calcite

OTHER COMPONENTS:
Fossil debris, clay, quartz

MATERIAL PROPORTIONS:
>50% dolomite

GRAIN SIZE:
Usually fine- to medium-grained

COLOUR:
Shades of brown, grey, yellowish or reddish

TEXTURAL FEATURES:
Usually even-textured, often poorly bedded, may be porous

DISTRIBUTION:
As for limestones

LOOKALIKES:
Limestone reacts more vigorously with acid

Dolomite

Chemical group: Carbonate

Dolomite shares the same name as the mineral (dolomite, *see* p.67) of which it is largely composed. In all other respects, it shares the same features as limestone. It reacts more slowly with acid than calcite-rich limestone, and is also often notably more dense. It may form during passage of water through ordinary limestone, when additional magnesium (required for the mineral dolomite) is fixed in the rock. All intermediate proportions of dolomite and calcite varieties of limestone are known. Dolomite may occur interbedded with limestone, and is more resistant to weathering. Found in the North of England, Jura/France, S Tyrol/Italy and the mountains of the same name, Dolomites/Italy.

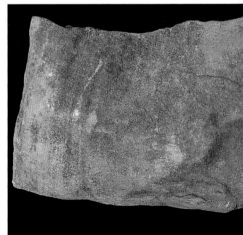

FAMILY: CHEMICAL SEDIMENT

ID FACT FILE

TYPICAL COMPONENTS:
Gypsum, anhydrite, halite

OTHER COMPONENTS:
Sylvite, clay

MATERIAL PROPORTIONS:
Variable

GRAIN SIZE:
Fine- to coarse-grained

COLOUR:
Often brightly coloured, reddish, yellowish, grey or white

TEXTURAL FEATURES:
Finely laminated, often massive and distorted or nodular

DISTRIBUTION:
Develop within shallow near-shoreline sedimentary basins around seas or in continental salt lakes

LOOKALIKES:
Soft distinctive minerals in coarse-grained varieties unlikely to be mistaken

Evaporite

Chemical group: Saline

Evaporites form by precipitation of minerals directly from water, during evaporation of trapped saline fluids, in trapped lagoons, salt lakes or intertidal zones, as at the Dead Sea between Israel and Jordan, and Great Salt Lake, Utah, USA. Precipitation is often cyclic and gives a banded or laminated appearance. Evaporite rocks are easily disturbed, and may be partly dissolved, leading to collapse and formation of angular pieces (breccia). Rocks of just one mineral type are common. Rock salt is composed almost entirely of halite, and gypsum rock is a variety of massive gypsum often with nodular or coarsely crystalline forms of twinned or fibrous gypsum. Substantial old evaporite deposits may represent lost seas. Found at Cheshire/England (Permian), Zechstein/Germany (Permian), Moscow Basin (Devonian) and the Dead Sea (Miocene):

Greywacke

Chemical group: Intermediate/acid

Greywacke has a characteristic very fine-grained matrix (silt-sized or mud) surrounding prominent sand-sized grains of quartz, lithic fragments and feldspar (mostly plagioclase). They can show sedimentary structures indicative of rapid accumulation and vigorous water currents. Indicators of enhanced tectonic or volcanic activity, they are often formed in basins. Found in Wales, Ireland, Southern Uplands/Scotland, Devon/England, Westphalia/Germany. They also form many of the Cretaceous-Tertiary erosional deposits in the Alps.

ID FACT FILE

TYPICAL COMPONENTS:
Quartz, feldspar, lithic fragments

OTHER COMPONENTS:
Haematite, mica, resistant minerals

MATERIAL PROPORTIONS:
Abundant quartz, feldspar and lithic fragments

GRAIN SIZE:
From very fine up to 2 mm

COLOUR:
Dark grey, greenish grey or black

TEXTURAL FEATURES:
Obvious quartz plus other mineral grains and rock fragments in a very fine-grained matrix (silt-sized); often bedded and graded

DISTRIBUTION:
Regional rock type associated with active geological periods of mountain building and volcanism

LOOKALIKES:
Dolerite

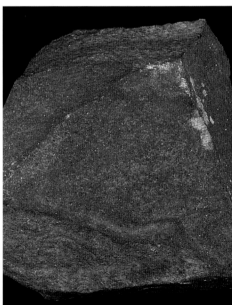

Ironstone

Chemical group: Intermediate/acid

Ancient ironstones often consist of banded haematite and magnetite layers interbedded with cherts and sandstones. They are an important economic source of iron. Younger oolitic ironstones often consist of rounded pellets called ooids cemented by haematite, goethite or siderite. Recent ironstones are represented by iron and manganese-rich nodules on the deep ocean floor. Ancient banded ironstones occur outside of Europe, as around Lake Superior/Canada, northwestern Australia and South Africa. Oolitic ironstones are found in Palaeozoic carbonate sediments as at S Wales, Northampton and Westbury/England, Lorraine/France, Luxembourg. *Ochre* is a brightly coloured red/yellow goethite/limonite-rich massive variety; *umber* is a finely laminated dark brown siltstone (*see* opposite). Umber and ochre occur with hydrothermal volcanic deposits from active seafloor spreading ridges as in the Cretaceous deposits of Cyprus.

FAMILY: IRON-RICH SEDIMENT

Ironstone Varieties
Chemical group: Intermediate/acid

red ochre

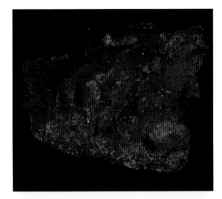

yellow ochre

umber

FAMILY: CARBONATE SEDIMENT

ID FACT FILE

TYPICAL COMPONENTS:
Calcite, fossil debris

OTHER COMPONENTS:
Dolomite, siderite, quartz, feldspar, mica, clay

MATERIAL PROPORTIONS:
Abundant calcite, up to ~95%

GRAIN SIZE:
From very fine mud to coarse gravel

COLOUR:
White, grey, yellowish, reddish, greenish or black

TEXTURAL FEATURES:
Usually bedded, often crowded with fossils

DISTRIBUTION:
Continental shelves, shallow seas, oceanic islands, lakes

LOOKALIKES:
Unlikely to be mistaken (except for dolomite); carbonate minerals react with acid

Limestone

Chemical group: Carbonate

Limestones are formed as biochemical or biological precipitates of carbonate minerals, and are very variable. They can form as carbonate muds, or from the accumulated carbonate-rich skeletons of fossils, as reefs, or in tidal flats. They may be porous, fine-grained or coarse-grained. The principle sources of the carbonates are the skeletons of many organisms including algae, corals, sponges, shelly fossils, crustacea and others. They can be subdivided on the basis of their grain shapes, or cements, or grain size. *Oolitic limestone* (*see* below) is a variety formed of rounded concretions that are less than 2 mm in size (ooids) and resemble fish eggs; it develops in shallow water. *Chalk* (*see* opposite) is a famous fine-grained white-coloured and often porous variety made from hard parts of algae and microfossils; it is sometimes associated with nodules of chert or flint. Reef limestone is an unbedded variety formed through continuous deposition of calcareous reef organisms like corals, algae, bryozoa, shelly fossils and sponges.

FAMILY: CARBONATE SEDIMENT

Limestone Variety: Chalk

Chemical group: Carbonate

FAMILY: SILICEOUS SEDIMENT

ID FACT FILE

TYPICAL COMPONENTS:
Silica, microfossils

OTHER COMPONENTS:
Minor clay, haematite

MATERIAL PROPORTIONS:
Mostly silica

GRAIN SIZE:
Fine- to medium-grained

COLOUR:
Grey, greenish or brownish

TEXTURAL FEATURES:
Dense rock, breaks with a brittle edge; abundant visible microfossils (may require hand lens)

DISTRIBUTION:
Exclusively seawater-derived; old rocks in mountain belts

LOOKALIKES:
Chert

Radiolarite

Chemical group: Acid

Radiolarite is a siliceous rock made of the skeletons of myriad siliceous microfossils called radiolaria. Soft siliceous muds or oozes are accumulating on the deep ocean floors today; radiolaria are common in equatorial regions. Occasional radiolarites contain microfossils that measure up to 3 mm, but the microfossils are usually much smaller and only clearly visible with a hand lens. Found at Bohemia/Czech Republic, Hohe Tauern/Austria, Corsica/France, Bavaria/Germany.

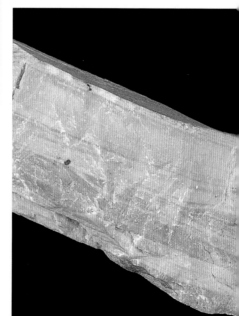

FAMILY: CLASTIC SEDIMENT

Sandstone

Chemical group: Acid

ID FACT FILE

TYPICAL COMPONENTS:
Quartz

OTHER COMPONENTS:
Calcite, feldspar, clay, mica, resistant minerals

MATERIAL PROPORTIONS:
Quartz dominant

GRAIN SIZE:
1/16 to 2 mm

COLOUR:
Whitish, grey, yellowish, red, brown

TEXTURAL FEATURES:
Prominent continuous layering due to bedding planes; sedimentary structures and indications of mechanical sorting of grains

DISTRIBUTION:
Widespread surface-formed regional rock type known from all different geological ages

LOOKALIKES:
Grades into siltstone (finer-grained) and conglomerates (coarser-grained)

Sandstone contains particles large enough to see with the naked eye and is always layered (bedding planes). It represents consolidated and cemented mechanical deposits of sands. Sands transported longer distances become richer in quartz, due to its hardness and resistance to weathering. Sandstone is often somewhat porous. Mechanical sorting (as for other clastic sediments) produces sandstone with a small range of grain sizes. Angular grains imply a short transportation distance. Sandstones represent old fluvial, deltaic and channel deposits and are frequently fossiliferous. Sandstone also occurs widely as wind-transported desert sands which often show cross bedding. It is a very popular building stone. Occurs in S Wales, the Midlands and the North of England, Midland Valley/Scotland, Rhine valley/Germany.

Sandstone Variety: Glauconitic Sandstone

Chemical group: Acid

ID FACT FILE

TYPICAL COMPONENTS:
Quartz

OTHER COMPONENTS:
Calcite, feldspar, clay, mica, resistant minerals

MATERIAL PROPORTIONS:
Quartz dominant; presence of glauconite

GRAIN SIZE:
$\frac{1}{16}$ to 2 mm

COLOUR:
Whitish, grey, yellowish, red, brown

TEXTURAL FEATURES:
Prominent continuous layering due to bedding planes; sedimentary structures and indications of mechanical sorting of grains

DISTRIBUTION:
Widespread surface-formed regional rock type known from all different geological ages

LOOKALIKES:
Grades into siltstone (finer-grained) and conglomerates (coarser-grained)

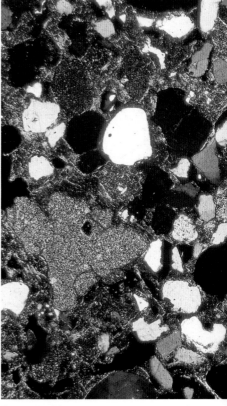

Petrographic thin section, view much enlarged (×25) shows rounded to angular quartz (white and grey) and irregular grains of glauconite (red and brown).

FAMILY: CLASTIC SEDIMENT

ID FACT FILE

TYPICAL COMPONENTS:
Clay, fine-grained silt

OTHER COMPONENTS:
Clay, quartz, mica, carbonate, organic compounds

MATERIAL PROPORTIONS:
>50% clay or rock powder (silt); may contain fossils

GRAIN SIZE:
Less than ¹⁄₁₆ mm

COLOUR:
Grey, brownish, greenish, reddish

TEXTURAL FEATURES:
Prominent partings, and fine laminations due to bedding planes; uniform appearance, sometimes with small rounded harder concretions or nodules

DISTRIBUTION:
Widespread; one of the commonest sedimentary rocks

LOOKALIKES:
Slate is much harder with cleavage

Shale

Chemical group: Intermediate/acid

Mudstones are the commonest sedimentary rocks. Shale is a consolidated variety of clay-rich mudstone with a well-developed parting, enabling it to split easily into thin sheets. For this property it is said to be 'fissile'. Mudstones are deposited in river flood plains, lakes, deltas, continental slopes and seafloors. Like mudstones in general, shale is easily weathered and produces subdued topography. Some shales include rounded nodules of carbonate minerals, pyrite or chert. Shale frequently occurs interbedded with coarser-grained sedimentary rocks, sometimes as regular repetitions forming sandstone-shale sequences. *Oil shale* is a dark grey or black variety rich in organic materials. *Marl* is a variety of mudstone that is rich in carbonates, formed as carbonate mud (*see* p.232). Found in N England, S Wales, S Scotland, France, Germany and most European countries.

FAMILY: CLASTIC SEDIMENT

ID FACT FILE

TYPICAL COMPONENTS:
Clay, fine-grained silt

OTHER COMPONENTS:
Clay, quartz, mica, carbonate, organic compounds

MATERIAL PROPORTIONS:
>50% clay or rock powder (silt); may contain fossils

GRAIN SIZE:
Less than $\frac{1}{16}$ mm

COLOUR:
Grey, brownish, greenish, reddish

TEXTURAL FEATURES:
Prominent partings, and fine laminations due to bedding planes; uniform appearance, sometimes with small rounded harder concretions or nodules

DISTRIBUTION:
Widespread; one of the commonest sedimentary rocks

LOOKALIKES:
Slate is much harder with cleavage

Shale Varieties

Chemical group: Intermediate/acid

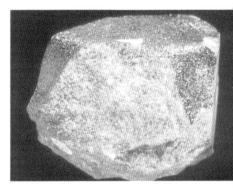

Marl

Oil shale

FAMILY: CARBONATE SEDIMENT

ID FACT FILE

TYPICAL COMPONENTS:
Calcite, dolomite

OTHER COMPONENTS:
Aragonite, minor clay

MATERIAL PROPORTIONS:
Mostly calcite

GRAIN SIZE:
Very fine-grained, no visible crystals

COLOUR:
Whitish, pale grey, pinkish, yellowish

TEXTURAL FEATURES:
Porous, irregular fine-scale banding

DISTRIBUTION:
Formed around hot springs

LOOKALIKES:
Marble, limestone

Travertine

Chemical group: Carbonate

Travertine is a porous variety of terrestrial limestone, formed as a chemical precipitate from waters emanating from hot springs. The fine laminations and banding reflect different growth layers. Can be almost pure calcite and, but for its high porosity, superficially resembles marble. Can also contain dolomite and aragonite, but these can be difficult to identify due to the very fine grain size. Found at Sabine Mountains/Central Italy, Württemburg and Thuringia/Germany.

FAMILY: IMPACTITE

Impactite

Chemical group: Silica-rich

Impactite is an extreme variety of metamorphic rock that forms by shock metamorphism (melting or anatexis) resulting from a large crater-forming impact. Pressures and temperatures are so high that the target rocks melt within seconds; some unmelted relics of crustal silicate rocks survive. Impactite can contain tiny diamonds formed by the shock pressure; sometimes feathery silicate textures (spinifex) occur. Impactite can form large bodies of glassy rock up to several kilometres in size; *tagamite* is the local name for impactite at the large 100-kilometre-diameter Popigai crater in Siberia. As for true volcanic glass, impactite glass weathers easily to clay minerals. Also found at Ries crater/S Germany, Chicxulub crater/Mexico, Charlevoix crater/Canada.

14-million-year-old impactite from Ries crater

Iron Meteorite

Chemical group: Iron-rich

ID FACT FILE

TYPICAL COMPONENTS:
Iron with nickel

OTHER COMPONENTS:
Graphite, troilite (FeS)

MATERIAL PROPORTIONS:
Mostly solid iron

COLOUR:
Metallic iron, dark distinctive crust; weathers brown

TEXTURAL FEATURES:
Fresh interior of metallic iron, when polished shows coarse elongated criss-crossing grains; may have small rounded inclusions of soft black graphite. The exterior is usually rusty brown with altered iron oxides/hydroxides and may be pitted and scalloped

TESTS:
Notable high density of nickel-iron (SG 6–7)

DISTRIBUTION:
A common class of meteorite, due to its resistance to weathering and ability to penetrate the Earth's atmosphere

LOOKALIKES:
Unlikely to be mistaken

All meteorites are rare; of these, iron meteorites are relatively common. They are coarsely crystalline alloys of iron and nickel (typically 7–15 per cent nickel), with small admixtures of additional trace metals, including gold and iridium. The crystalline textures revealed on prepared smooth surfaces etched with acid are known as *Widmanstatten* structure; it can only be produced by very slow cooling, perhaps in parent asteroids a few hundred kilometres in size. Iron meteorites were all formed within a short period of time of the birth of the Solar System around 4,550 million years ago. *Hexahedrite* is a variety with low nickel (~7%), *octahedrite* has high nickel (~40%) and *ataxite* is nickel-rich but lacks the Widmanstatten structure perhaps as a result of reheating.

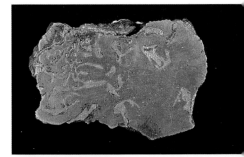

FAMILY: MARTIAN METEORITE ('SNC')

ID FACT FILE

ESSENTIAL MINERALS:
Olivine, diopside, enstatite, plagioclase

OTHER MINERALS:
Carbonate, glass, spinel

COLOUR:
Green, black, grey

TEXTURAL FEATURES:
Medium- to coarse-grained silicate minerals with interlocking igneous rock textures

TESTS:
Laboratory tests reveal anomalously very young ages for meteorites

DISTRIBUTION:
Rare class of meteorite

LOOKALIKES:
Gabbro, dunite, lherzolite, picrite

Martian Meteorite

Chemical group: Silicate-rich; basic/ultrabasic

Martian meteorites are made of the same silicate minerals that occur on Earth, and resemble basic igneous rocks, although some also contain unusual black glass formed by shock melting. Unlike most other meteorites, which have ages of 4,550 millon years, these are very young with ages to 180 million years. One famous Martian meteorite contains small microscopic shapes in carbonate minerals, which resemble microfossils; this meteorite (ALH84001, illustrated) provided in 1996 the first evidence for a 'fossilized Martian biota'. As with most meteorites, Martian meteorites often have a distinctive black *fusion crust*.

Stony Meteorite

Chemical group: Silicate-rich

ID FACT FILE

ESSENTIAL MINERALS:
Pyroxene, olivine
or plagioclase

OTHER MINERALS:
Nickel-rich iron,
graphite, spinel,
chromite

COLOUR:
Dark grey,
greenish, black;
mottled

TEXTURAL FEATURES:
Fine-grained
silicate minerals,
often with small
pea-sized
rounded
inclusions
(chondrules).
Matrix can be
very fine-grained,
sometimes with
fragments of
glass or metallic
iron

TESTS:
Dark crusty
surface texture
can be
distinctive

DISTRIBUTION:
The most
abundant class
of meteorite

LOOKALIKES:
Similar to fine-
grained gabbro,
peridotite, picrite

All meteorites are rare; stony meteorites are the most common family. Most meteorites have a dark 'rind' or fusion crust caused by heating during flight through the atmosphere. They are made of the same silicate minerals (bronzite, diopside, olivine and plagioclase) that occur in terrestrial gabbro, plus occasional glass and small amounts of nickel-rich iron. Most of them contain rounded *chondrules* in a fine-grained matrix, sometimes with fragments of glass or metallic nickel-iron and are called *chondrites*; those without are much less common and are called *achondrites*. They contain small amounts of microscopic diamonds.

FAMILY: STONY-IRON METEORITE

Stony-iron Meteorite

Chemical group: Silicate and iron metal

All meteorites are rare; the stony-iron meteorites are the most rare (less than 10 per cent). They are mixtures of silicate minerals (dark-coloured bronzite, diopside, olivine and whitish-coloured plagioclase) and substantial amounts of nickel-rich iron. *Mesosiderite* contains chunks of nickel-iron metal, angular fragments of silicate rock (bronzite, olivine and plagioclase), glass and metal veins. *Pallasite* contains large, often gem-quality olivines (peridote) up to 1 cm in size in a connected metal matrix; these are thought to have come from the cores of large asteroids like Vesta (500 km in size). The photograph shows pallasite; the pale hollows are eroded olivines.

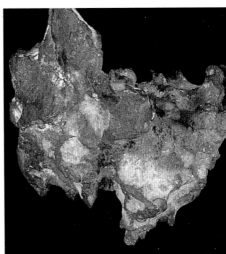

FAMILY: IMPACTITE

Suevite

Chemical group: Silica-rich or carbonate-rich

TYPICAL COMPONENTS:
Silicate rock fragments and impact glass (may be altered)

OTHER COMPONENTS:
Any

COLOUR:
Grey, speckled, greenish, brownish, dark

TEXTURAL FEATURES:
Angular fragments of all sizes of rocks and minerals, including dark fragments of partly porous glass, in a fine-grained matrix. Usually silicate-rich or carbonate-rich. Sometimes layered or bedded; occasional levels of impact lapilli (*see* tuff; p.175)

TESTS:
Association with impact crater features

DISTRIBUTION:
Rare rock but occurs within large impact craters (>approx 20 km)

LOOKALIKES:
Breccia, ignimbrite, tuff

Suevites are mixed rocks containing some dispersed impact melt. They are composed of fragments of partly porous impact glass, glass bombs, numerous fragments of crystalline and sedimentary rocks in a matrix of the same materials but finer-grained. Some rock fragments are highly shocked, others are barely affected; even fossils may be preserved. They may contain tiny diamonds and other minerals indicative of very high shock pressure, such as coesite and stishovite (*see* quartz; p.124). Found at Ries crater/S Germany, Popigai crater/Siberia, Chicxulub crater/Mexico, Haughton crater/Canada. The photograph is of suevite from the Ries crater.

FAMILY: TEKTITE

ID FACT FILE

TYPICAL COMPONENTS:
Glass

OTHER COMPONENTS:
Usually none

COLOUR:
Black, yellowish, brown, green

TEXTURAL FEATURES:
Smooth rounded shapes, sometimes flattened, with distinctive pitted, grooved or fluted surfaces

TESTS:
Conchoidal fracture. Translucent to transparent in thin flakes

DISTRIBUTION:
Very widespread as clasts in both continental and oceanic sediments; restricted in age to youngish rocks (Tertiary–Recent)

LOOKALIKES:
Volcanic glass, obsidian

Tektite

Chemical group: Acid

Tektites occur as vast sprayed fields of liquid melted rock that has been jetted from large meteorite impacts within continental crust. Their shapes form as tear-shaped drops with viscous draglines on the surface (the grooves and flutes). They are very rich in silica; thin flakes are translucent to transparent and show their true colours. They are named after the regions in which they occur, such as *thailandite* (Thailand), *australasite* (Australia) and georgite (Georgia/USA). *Moldavite* is a bottle-green variety from Moldavia/Czechoslovakia related to the 25-km diameter Ries impact crater in southern Germany (age 15 million years) that lies 400 km away.

INDEX

Main entries are given in **bold**.